Northern Rail Steam

6604
75009

Northern Rail Steam

The Final Years

Allan Heyes

www.crecy.co.uk

ISBN 9781800352520

First published in 2022 by Crécy Publishing Ltd

A CIP record for this book is available from the British Library

Printed in Turkey by Pelikan Print

Crécy Publishing Limited
1a Ringway Trading Estate
Shadowmoss Road
Manchester M22 5LH

www.crecy.co.uk

Front cover: On 1 April 1965 Britannia Pacifics meet at Springs Branch. No. 70028, formerly named *Royal Star,* is working a southbound freight; No. 70023, formerly named *Venus*, heads north on a Euston-Windermere train.

Rear cover main: 9F No. 92018 passing through Pocket Nook Junction, St. Helens, with a Long Meg-Widnes anhydrite train in March 1967.

Inset upper left: On 4 March 1967 *Clun Castle* is serviced at Chester Midland shed before returning with The Zulu as far as Banbury.

Inset upper: Passing Boars Head Junction, Black 5 No. 45347 climbs out of Wigan with a northbound parcels train in July 1967.

Inset middle: It's early morning on 21 September 1965 at Winstanley Colliery Sidings as Black 5 No. 45239 climbs Orrell Bank with the 07.18 Bolton to Liverpool Exchange local.

Inset bottom: Black 5 No. 44800 provides vigorous rear end assistance to E.E. Type 4 No. D224 *Lucania* over Whalley Viaduct with a Long Meg-Widnes anhydrite train on 15 October 1967.

Half title page: The sun is partially obscured by the exhaust of Black 5 No. 44679, employed on station pilot duties at Wigan North Western on 30 December 1966.

Page 2: Collett 0-6-2T No. 6604 and, lurking in the shadows, Standard 4MT No. 75009, await their next turn of duty at Wrexham's Croes Newydd shed on 16 July 1964.

Title page: It's well below freezing point at Springs Branch on the morning of 28 December 1967 and water dribbling from the leaking tender of an unidentified withdrawn 8F has created this display of icicles. The depot had closed on 4 December, resulting in the withdrawal of most of its steam allocation.

Contents page: A busy scene at Clitheroe on 14 February 1967. After shunting the yard, Fairburn Class 4 2-6-4T No. 42297 takes water before returning to Blackburn.

Contents

The penultimate Black 5 No. 44686 is working the 12.15 Wigan to Liverpool Exchange stopper. The home signal beyond the bridge is Winstanley Colliery Siding's down starter with Orrell East's distant beneath.

Dedication

To the vast numbers of men and women, volunteers and professionals, who keep the steam locomotive alive today on the main lines and preserve the steam age environment on our heritage railways.

Acknowledgments

I have referred to several publications during the preparation of this work, including Hugh Longworth's *British Steam Locomotives 1948—1968 and BR Steam Locomotives Complete Allocations History 1948—1968* (OPC); *BR Main Line Gradient Profiles, The Age of Steam* (Ian Allan) and various websites, including Wikipedia.

I must also thank Steven Leyland, Neville Hopkins and Mike Taylor for providing some of the more obscure details of locations, locomotives, rosters and signalling.

Introduction

This book may be regarded as a sequel to *Northern Rail Rover*, taking an alternative view of the final years of steam operation in Northern England on the main line and in industry. Using my personal photographic record, sequences of pictures are used to recreate the lineside experience in the 1960s. There is no attempt to glamorise the subject – locomotives nearing the end of their lives are seen in their working environment, as are the people involved in operating them. Diesel and electric motive power was becoming increasingly dominant in this environment and cannot be ignored; therefore a few pictures, now of considerable historical interest, are included. Industrial steam was also in sharp decline in the 1960s, but it did last for quite a long time after the demise of main line steam. Consequently, a few pictures taken as late as the mid-1970s are also included.

For the purposes of this work, the boundary of the North Country has been extended southwards to Wrexham. Chapter 1 begins with a visit to Wrexham's Croes Newydd shed in July 1964, followed by a sequence of pictures taken within a couple of hours on Gresford Bank. Unfortunately, ex- GWR motive power was in decline by this time and the Shrewsbury to Chester route had been moved into the London Midland Region, so ex-LMS locos had become dominant by 1964.

Various locations in Liverpool and South West Lancashire appear in Chapter 2 before following the LYR line towards Wigan.

In Chapter 3 my home area of Wigan, often overlooked as a major railway centre, is covered in some detail. Three of the 'Big Four' had stations there, although the ex-GCR Central closed in November 1964. The LYR provided services from Wallgate Station to Liverpool, Southport, Manchester and Yorkshire, which continued until the end of the steam era and beyond. From the nearby North Western Station the LNWR provided services to London, Scotland and the Midlands, also competing with the LYR with connections to Liverpool and Manchester. Their route to Liverpool via St. Helens is now electrified but the Manchester line via Tyldesley was closed long ago. Winstanley Colliery Sidings, a favourite spot on the LYR route to Liverpool, was very close to home and is therefore seen in some detail. Unfortunately, by the mid-1960s, there was very little freight on this line and much of the passenger services were provided by DMUs. Memories go back to the 1950s and the seemingly constant procession of freight from Yorkshire, the Manchester area and even the Midlands, almost all heading for Merseyside docks and all requiring banking, usually a 4F, up the 1 in 91 gradient.

Springs Branch shed, which ceased steam operation on 4 December 1967, was the largest depot in the Wigan area, outlasting both the GCR Lower Ince (closed in the early 1950s) and the LYR (closed in mid-1964) sheds. A new facility has opened recently for the stabling and maintenance of modern traction units.

There was no really fast running on the main line around Wigan in steam days due to the rather uncertain effects of mining subsidence; the main operational interest was the ascent of the 1 in 104 gradient north to Boars Head Junction. This was the steepest gradient faced by trains from Euston after topping Camden Bank almost 200 miles to the south. Slow moving freights on this section, which was double track only, were a problem at busy times. The answer was the Whelley Line, allowing trains from Bamfurlong to the south to pass east of Wigan and re-join the main line at Standish Junction. This line, and all its complex junctions at the south end, was completed in the 1880s. Before leaving the Wigan area it must be recorded that steam was still active at Bickershaw Collieries long after it had finished on the main lines. A picture taken on 17 September 1976 is included but steam did continue for some time after this.

Moving on to South East Lancashire and Chapter 4 there is, first of all, a look at a pair of the Horwich Works shunters about a month before their withdrawal. At this time the ex-LYR saddletank, still carrying its LMS number, 11305, was the oldest locomotive on the BR stock list. The next location is Bolton, which retained a strong LYR atmosphere in the 1960s, reflected in the electro-pneumatic signalling system at Bolton West and the station buildings, which date back to Victorian and Edwardian times. Before leaving this area, the variety of industrial steam is portrayed – where steam and even electric motive power was active alongside main line steam.

The start of Chapter 5 is marked by crossing the border into Yorkshire, where Holbeck Jubilees are seen at Long Preston, Skipton and on their home shed. There is also a picture of historical interest taken at the site of first Hellifield Station. Most of the pictures taken in the North East are the product of seven-day Northern Rail Rover tickets in the summers of 1966 and 1967.

The possibilities of rail travel in the summer of 1967 are highlighted in Chapter 6, which makes use of copious diary notes and photos taken over seven days from the end of June into early July. Many of these journeys are no longer possible and many more certainly not at the nocturnal 1967 times. This chapter forms a centrepiece of the book, but many of these pictures would not have been possible just two months later, when steam operation had ceased on the North Eastern Region.

Moving west across another border into Cumbria, Chapter 7 begins at Carlisle followed by a brief interlude around Shap. The main content of this chapter is, however, a survey of the industrial scene, firstly at the British Gypsum works near Cumwhinton and then along the Cumbrian Coast, where steam was still active into the 1970s. The steam locomotive was invented primarily to serve industry and it is fitting that its last commercial use was also in an industrial setting.

Chapter 8 is certainly a trip down memory lane for the author! A summer Saturday afternoon on the lineside at Euxton Junction, a few miles south of Preston, is re-enacted using 10 pictures taken over a period of about 3 hours. There were, in fact, 12 steam-hauled trains during this time and the 10 pictures suffice to illustrate most of the possible paths through the junction where the line from Manchester meets the West Coast Main Line. The basic layout of the junction and the pathing options are largely unchanged today although diamond crossings have, unsurprisingly, been eliminated.

The general appearance of Preston Station has not changed very much since steam days and this is well illustrated in Chapter 9. The most obvious changes are the elimination of the old East Lancashire Railway approaches and the closure to the public of the western island platform. It is always worth recalling that the last two scheduled steam-hauled passenger trains departed from Preston on 3 August 1968. The 20.50 to Blackpool, hauled by Black 5 No.45212, was the rear portion of the 17.05 from Euston and finally, the 21.25 to Liverpool, a portion of the 17.25 from Glasgow, left behind Black 5 No.45318.

It was difficult to see how BR could function without steam around Blackburn right up to August 1968. This is illustrated in Chapter 10 with some steam pictures taken as late as 16 July, with no diesel locomotive sightings recorded on this occasion.

Continuing into East Lancashire, Chapter 11 begins in the pastoral environment of the Ribble Valley and illustrates the transition from steam to diesel traction, now approaching completion. For the author there is certainly some satisfaction to be gained from the sight of an English Electric Type 4 diesel needing assistance from a Black 5 on the climb from Whalley to Wilpshire! There was steam shunting at Clitheroe right up to The End and this is shown in some detail. The surprising discovery of an electrified railway in Clitheroe is also pictured, at the gasworks of all places!

The Epilogue is not a requiem for steam. The massive public interest in the end of steam specials of August 1968 is seen as a portent of the remarkable resurgence of main line steam, which continues unabated in 2022. The preparation of this book has allowed me to rekindle many treasured memories, which, I hope can be shared, especially by older readers. For enthusiasts too young to remember, the realities of the steam age are, hopefully, brought to life.

Since August 1968 an enormous number of 'steam miles' have been run in the UK and a heartfelt thanks must be extended to all who have made this possible.

Allan Heyes
March 2022

Black 5 No. 44776 will spend the night of 16—17 June 1967 shunting parcels vans at Wigan North Western Station, the open firebox door also providing some welcome warmth on a chilly evening.

Chapter One Wrexham to Chester and the Wirral

The weather forecast is good for 16 July 1964. At an average cycling speed of 10/12mph, the ETA at Wrexham's Croes Newydd shed, 43 miles from home in Wigan, is around 11.00. Arrival is on time to find four locomotives having a late morning siesta in the roundhouse. Dating from 1902, the shed is the last of the GWR 'Northlight' designs to be built, closing to steam on 5 June 1967.

All the locomotives were, appropriately, built at Swindon. On the right is Collett 0-6-2T No.6604 of 1927. Lurking in the shadows on the left is Hawksworth 0-6-0PT No. 1628 of 1950, which can be regarded as one of the very last standard gauge GWR locos to work on BR, even though it was built after nationalisation; withdrawal was in September 1966. All 80 of the BR Class 4 4-6-0s in the 75XXX series were built at Swindon. 75009, nearest the camera, worked until August 1968 at Carnforth. No. 75026 ended its life as one of the Shap bankers at Tebay.

It's only a short distance to the ex-GWR Wrexham Station and BR Standard Class 5 No. 73090 soon appears on the 08.20 Paddington—Chester, described in the public timetable as 'Inter City'. The fine bracket signal indicates the complexity of the lines north of the station where the ex-GCR lines run parallel to the ex-GWR before descending to the Central Station. This basic layout remains unchanged in 2022, the line from Central providing a service to the Wirral area.

Time for a snack in the buffet before the short ride to the top of Gresford Bank, where the exchange sidings for the colliery are situated. The following five pictures were taken within a couple of hours in the afternoon on 16 July 1964.

The fireman of 8F No. 48632 has perhaps been a little over-active, producing a great pall of black smoke and an excess of steam, even at the top of the bank. No. 48632, a Mold Junction loco heading a southbound freight, appears to be in fine fettle, fairly clean and steamtight.

Shortly after this spectacular performance the view to the south reveals, unsurprisingly, a lineside fire. A common occurrence, this will be left to burn itself out. Ivatt Mogul No. 46509, a locomotive with GWR associations, is waiting to head north from the colliery exchange sidings with a short freight. Swindon built the last 25 of these LMS-designed locos between November 1952 and March 1953, all of which worked in the Western Region until wider dispersal towards the end of their lives. Black 5 No. 45399, working a Liverpool—Paddington special, comes into the picture with a demonstration of more efficient working than 48632!

No. 46509 has now left the sidings and is checked by signals down the bank as No. 73090 appears on its return working, the 14.30 Chester—Paddington 'Inter City'. Allocated to Shrewsbury at this time, it must have had a quick turn round at Chester, probably not needing coaling before returning to its home shed. Hauling six coaches up the 1 in 82 gradient is no problem for No. 73090 and the summit of the Chester—Shrewsbury line, just south of Chirk, is only a little higher than this point. The sawtooth gradient profile will produce some high speeds in the dips.

Following closely behind is a very grimy Black 5 No. 45130 on a fitted freight. It is coping very well with the gradient and, indeed, no banking was seen all afternoon. The track layout, combined with comprehensive signalling, allows direct access into the exchange sidings from up and down lines and there even appears to be route indicators on the signals in the sidings. The structure in the distance takes spoil from the colliery to a tip just out of the picture on the left. Gresford Colliery closed in 1973.

Time to move on now, explore down the bank and get a bit nearer to home. The unmistakeable sound of a GWR vacuum pump is heard and there are just a few seconds to snatch this shot of Hall No. 6922 *Burton Hall*, a Shrewsbury loco, coasting down the bank on the 12.10 Paddington—Birkenhead. Shrewsbury had been absorbed into the London Midland Region, coded 6D, from September 1963, Croes Newydd becoming 6C at the same time; 6D had a large and varied allocation of Class 5 power: Black 5s, Halls and 73XXXs. Time to head north again; ETA in Wigan 21.30, total distance covered about 105 miles and expenses in steam-age currency about half a crown!

Fast forward from 16 July 1964 to 12 August 1971 and a reminder that steam was still active in the Wrexham area long after the end of steam on BR in August 1968. *Hornet,* a Peckett 0-4-0ST Works No. 1935, built 1937, is working at Bersham Colliery, about 1½ miles south of Wrexham. However, coal mining and its associated steam activity was also in sharp decline by this time and Bersham was the last of more than 30 collieries once in this area, sunk in 1864 and closing in December 1986.

Back now to 30 August 1966 and the scene at the eastern end of Chester Station. Apart from the presence of a 9F, this scene is unlikely to have changed very much for 40 years. Most of the signalling is of LNWR origin, reflecting the importance of Chester on its Euston—Holyhead route. No. 92105 of Birkenhead is in charge of a train of oil tanks from the Ellesmere Port area. It appears to be heading for the Warrington line and, if so, will shortly be faced with just over a mile of climbing at 1 in 100 and the fireman is now preparing for this.

On 4 March 1967, Ian Allan marked the end of the Paddington—Birkenhead though services by chartering two special runs over this route. The Chester GWR depot had been absorbed into the London Midland Region as early as February 1958 and recoded 6E (from 84K) and closed on 10 April 1960. Northgate shed had closed in January of that year, leaving only the Midland shed to deal with all locomotive servicing.

While BR Standard 5MT No. 73026 is taking its train to Birkenhead, some really dirty work must be done on *Clun Castle*, allowing a look into the smokebox. Emerging from Swindon Works in May 1950, it is one of the 7000-series Castles fitted with mechanical lubricators, No. 7029 also being fitted with a 4-row superheater and double chimney by October 1959.

Was this the first time that two Castles had been seen simultaneously in Chester Midland shed? Both now appear to be ready for their return runs, with No. 7029 having the shorter trip to Banbury. No. 4079 *Pendennis Castle* has been restored to its original 1924 condition and is still remarkably clean after its longer trip from Didcot on the 'Birkenhead Flier', No. 73035 taking the train on to Birkenhead.

This picture serves as a reminder that Castles were built at Swindon over a period of 27 years, the first in 1923 and the last in August 1950, numbered No. 7037 and appropriately named *Swindon.* An overhaul of No. 4079 has recently been completed, although reportedly not with a view to mainline running.

4079

A little while later, around 50 yards down the line, the sun is shining for the departure of 'The Zulu'. No. 7029 is proudly displaying its Great Western ancestry – although dating only from May 1950, it was never owned by the GWR! Its recent restoration for main-line running has seen a return to BR green livery, complete with appropriate crest and smokebox number plate. The road out of Chester is downhill at this point, where No. 7029 will shortly pass the racecourse, cross over the River Dee, but then by climbing Gresford Bank must lift the train out of the Dee Valley before reaching Wrexham.

Opposite: Pendennis Castle leaves Chester on the return run to Didcot. It has a longer run than No. 7029, was the second arrival, and is the first departure. The load is 11 coaches, which will demand quite a big effort on the 1 in 82 of Gresford Bank about seven miles ahead, giving the fireman ample preparation time.

Before leaving this area, a look at a typical photo stop in steam days: the date is 22 October 1966, at Ellesmere Port. Officialdom would usually turn a blind eye to the often risky behaviour of passengers on these occasions! Britannia Pacific No. 70004 *William Shakespeare* has lost its nameplate but is quite clean, probably the work of enthusiasts at its home depot, Stockport. This tour started at Liverpool Riverside Station hauled by Class 4 2-6-4T No. 42233, assisted by Black 5 No. 45015 to Edge Hill. No. 70004 took over at Manchester for the longer run to Birkenhead with Crab No. 42942 completing the tour at Liverpool Central.

Chapter Two — South West Lancashire

There are contrasts in motive power at Liverpool Lime Street Station on 13 May 1964 as Bo-Bo electric loco No. E3081 leaves with the 09.40 to Bournemouth. A hundred broadly similar locomotives were introduced between 1959 and 1963 from a variety of sources. All were Bo-Bos of 3,300 total horsepower, E3081 being one of 20 introduced by BR in 1962. It will certainly not need banking assistance up the 1 in 93 gradient to Edge Hill from Jinty No. 47487, which, as station pilot, can stand aside and deal with empty coaching stock and parcels traffic as required.

The scene at Edge Lane Junction on 9 June 1965: 8F No. 48078 is coming off the Bootle Branch and heading towards the sidings at Edge Hill. The alternative route eastwards to Olive Mount Junction is now reinstated after closure for many years. The Bootle Branch, connecting with the thriving docklands north of Pierhead, is now well used, carrying biomass, steel, scrap metal and containers. The bridge beyond the signal box carries Binns Road, the location of the Meccano/Hornby factory at this time, over the railway.

Black 5 No. 45107 is leaving Liverpool Exchange Station with a train of empty coaching stock on 13 May 1964. The enormous No. 2 Signal Box, built by the Lancashire and Yorkshire Railway, has a 168-lever frame and earned a place in railway history in the late evening of Saturday 3 August 1968. Some of these levers were pulled to allow the last regular steam-hauled train run by BR into the station, the 21.25 from Preston, hauled by Black 5 No. 45318. By 1977 long distance trains had ceased to use the station and the box closed on 2 April of that year after the electrified lines had been diverted into the underground network nearby, rendering Exchange Station redundant.

The former West Lancashire Railway route from Southport to Preston is due to close in early September 1964. Three trains leave Southport between 08.29 and 09.30, so it is well worth making the easy 20-mile ride to Banks on a fine sunny morning. Fowler Class 4 2-6-4T No. 42369 working the 08.50 stopper from Southport, as it accelerates briskly away with only three coaches and very few passengers on 1 September.

The LYR took over the struggling WLR in 1897 and in 1900 completed a spur south of Preston to give access to the East Lancashire side of the station, so allowing the closure of the WLR Fishergate Hill Station to passengers, but not for goods and parcels until 1965.

Opposite: March 1967: the location is Pocket Nook Junction at the eastern approaches to St. Helens. Kingmoor 9F No. 92018 is nearing the end of its long journey from Long Meg to Widnes with one of the regular anhydrite trains as it cautiously negotiates the reverse curves from Gerards Bridge Junction. It will shortly pass through the station and take the Widnes line at the platform end, although the line on the right would offer a more direct route avoiding the station. No. 92018 has come via Ais Gill, Hellifield, Blackburn, and the Wigan avoiding line (the Whelley line). The smokebox number plate has probably become a collector's item by this time!

Rainford Junction on Sunday 5 May 1963. The very sparse Sunday service on the Wigan—Liverpool Exchange line did, however, produce some exotic motive power! B1 No. 61276 is a long way from its home at York as it pulls away with the afternoon 'slow' train, leaving Wigan at 14.51. The St. Helens platform in the foreground, although very tidy, has not been used since June 1951.

Note the LYR signal to the left of the signal box, a structure dating from 1933 with 56 levers at this time. Now, only 10 of these suffice as the line has been singled on to Kirkby and the junction is no more.

Opposite: Fowler 2-6-4T No. 42374, a Springs Branch loco on 15 July 1965, has restarted the 18.05 Liverpool—Wigan local from Upholland, about a quarter of a mile back. The 1 in 114 gradient will soon level out for the 959-yard passage through the tunnel that marks the summit of this route. Two stops to go, Orrell and Pemberton, and it's virtually all downhill to Wigan Wallgate.

The ex-LYR shed at Wigan had closed in April 1964 and Springs Branch locos subsequently became common on all lines around Wigan.

Chapter Three The Wigan Area

No. 43945, a 4F 0-6-0 built for the Midland Railway by Armstrong Whitworth in 1921 and still going strong on 7 July 1960, passes Orrell West signal box. Heading for Merseyside, it will soon enter Upholland Tunnel about a quarter of a mile ahead, the banker, another 4F, dropping off opposite the box.

The first Upholland Station, dating from 20 November 1848, was at this location, the present Upholland Station being named Pimbo Lane at that time. Closure came very soon, around September 1852, probably because it was only about half a mile from the alternative station at Orrell.

Opposite: It's a rather gloomy damp morning on 28 December 1966 as Black 5 No. 44809 emerges from the eastern portal of Upholland Tunnel on the daily Fazakerley—Bamfurlong freight. Only a breath of steam is needed to keep the train moving on the level through the tunnel but the driver will soon close the regulator for the descent to Wigan Wallgate, mostly down gradients of around 1 in 90.

No. 44809 was a well-travelled loco, having been reallocated no less than 12 times by BR since 1948!

It's about 8am at Winstanley Colliery Sidings as the sun breaks through the early-morning mist. Black 5 No. 45239 has left Bolton at 07.18 and Wigan at 07.51 for a leisurely run to Liverpool on a 'stopper' with only three coaches in tow. The first stop out of Wigan has been Pemberton, where it has had to restart on the 1 in 90 gradient, which is maintained for about two miles to Orrell West. The date is 21 September 1965.

Another look at Winstanley Colliery Sidings and the daily Fazakerley—Bamfurlong freight, on this occasion, 30 March 1967, worked by Aintree 8F No. 48676. The actual colliery sidings, which probably went out of use and were removed in the early 1930s, connected with the loop on the left beyond the signal box, which, nevertheless, retained its original name until its closure in 1967. Aintree shed closed in June 1967, resulting in the loss of one of the last regular steam rosters and the virtual elimination of steam from this route. The loops, extending from Winstanley to Orrell East, became redundant and their days numbered.

Seen from exactly the same spot on the same day, 30 March 1967, No. 48676 is working its return run from Bamfurlong to Fazakerley. It has left the West Coast Main Line immediately south of Wigan North Western Station to access the ex-LYR lines and pass through the Wallgate Station. A brief stop has allowed the banker, another 8F, to buffer up and assist for the climb to Upholland Tunnel. Note the sign on the right marking the location of catch points that would derail any vehicles running away down the gradient. The sack on the front of the loco will probably be retrieved by the crew when back on Aintree shed, contents unknown.

Moving on to 8 June 1967 and a last look at Winstanley Colliery Sidings. The signal box, a replacement of the LYR original, was built by the LMSR in 1947 with a 25-lever frame and was closed on 17 December 1967. The LYR water tower must be at least 24 years older and was, with the loops, put out of use at this time.

A DMU, forming the 18.30 express from Liverpool Exchange to Manchester, Bradford and Leeds, also gets into the picture. Note the fogman's concrete hut and the apparatus he would use to place detonators on the line a few yards in front of the DMU.

42711

Black 5 No. 44734 is working the summer Saturday 13.30 Liverpool—Manchester on 18 July 1964. Signalled to take the Wigan line at Pemberton Junction, it is at the point where the gradient steepens from 1 in 90 and braking hard to take the junction at around 40mph. The smell of hot cast iron and steel will linger in the air for quite a while!

No. 44734 was built at Crewe by BR in February 1949 and spent all its working life at Newton Heath; did they ever clean it?

Opposite: Horwich Crab No. 42711, an Aintree loco at this time, approaches Pemberton Station on 4 January 1961, probably on the familiar Bamfurlong—Fazakerley freight. The line appears to level out at this point, but this is an illusion. The gradient simply eases to 1 in 90 for the next two miles or so. Did anyone know the actual gradient(s) between Pemberton Junction and the station? The track diagram in the signal box said 1 in 45, figures of 1 in 63 and 93 have appeared in print, and there was certainly a gradient post reading of 1 in 39 just out of this picture on the right!

The flimsy-looking gas lamp is the only concession to passenger safety but it does appear to be in good working order.

Manchester United fans may wish to skip over this picture and caption. 23 April 1966 was a memorable day for Everton supporters when their team beat Manchester United at Bolton's Burnden Park to reach the final of the FA Cup. BR ran several special trains, all but one travelling over the Westwood Park Line to avoid Wigan. Once a busy passenger and freight route, it had lost almost all its regular traffic by this time. Black 5 No. 45034 is approaching Pemberton Junction as it returns the jubilant Everton fans to Merseyside. The engine crew, however, will be more concerned with the task of hauling 10 well-filled coaches up the severe gradients to Upholland Tunnel in very wet weather.

Repeater signals were a common sight in steam days, the upper arm offering a clear view against the sky. Everton won the FA Cup at Wembley.

The LYR was anxious to compete with the LNWR and CLC for the lucrative Manchester—Liverpool traffic and completed the Wigan Avoiding Line by the summer of 1889, so avoiding a severe slack to pass through Wallgate Station. Before very long a 40-minute timing between the two cities could be offered, which was not bettered by its rivals.

The 08.30 departure from Liverpool was the last train to use the line, seen here on 31 March 1967, crossing the Leigh branch of the Leeds—Liverpool Canal at Westwood Park. This train ran this way until the closure of the line on 14 July 1969 and was subsequently diverted through Wigan Wallgate. Dominating the background are the cooling towers of Westwood Power Station, 314 feet high and demolished on 15 January 1989.

Now moving eastwards from Westwood Park to Hindley where an 8F is seen working a train of coal empties from Fazakerley to Crofton. Hindley No. 2 signal box, dating back to 1887, has 80 levers and controls four running lines, loops, various crossovers and the junction for the spur to De Trafford Junction on the Whelley line. The signal for this route is pulled off, one of 15 on this magnificent gantry. The 8F, which is hiding its identity beneath a thick layer of grime, will take the Bolton line at Crow Nest Junction and then go via Castleton, so avoiding Manchester. There are now only two tracks at this location running through an avenue of trees.

Wigan Wallgate Station on 30 July 1964: Ivatt Class 2 2-6-0 No. 46444 approaches with the 12.40 Liverpool to Rochdale local. No. 46444 is one the many LMS-designed locos built by BR, in this case at Crewe in February 1950, Nos. 46400—46464 having the shorter LMS pattern chimney. The present station dates from 2 February 1896 and is not the first which was situated closer to the LNWR station on the other side of the short tunnel under Wallgate. Around 1855 it was moved to a position within this field of view on the right, which sufficed for another 41 years. Some of the infrastructure, such as the water tower and gas lamps, may well have been in use for 60 years or more!

A pair of Springs Branch Black 5s, performing menial tasks, dominate this picture taken from the island platform of Wigan Wallgate Station. In the background No. 45321 is on pilot duties at the main line station and No. 44962 is shunting the LYR goods yard. The gradient post in the foreground is a reminder that the L&Y line must climb sharply to the same level as the main line within a few hundred yards, a potentially difficult start for Manchester or Bolton trains. The varied assortment of road vehicles adds interest to the picture and, unlike the Black 5s, they all look very clean! The date is 18 April 1967.

On 18 June 1967 Black 5 No. 45374, a Carnforth loco, has a brief encounter with No. 45149 from Lostock Hall at Wigan No.2 signal box as it recovers from a signal check with a southbound freight. Note that No. 45149 has the earlier design of the so-called domeless boiler fitted to the first 225 Black 5s, BR Nos. 45000—45224, and No. 45374 has the later type, with separate dome and top feed. The signal box, constructed during the Second World War as part of a resignalling scheme, is an ARP design. It has minimal window area as well as very thick walls and roof to withstand anything other than a direct bomb blast.

Moving on now to a line that closed to passengers in November 1964, long before the end of steam. D7586 is unusual motive power for the 09.00 Wigan Central to Manchester Central. It is passing Wigan Goods, the location of the first Great Central Railway station in Wigan, opened in April 1884, the extension to Central Station dating from October 1892. The turntable was probably installed when the first station was built and has certainly not been used for a long time before this picture was taken on 31 August 1964. Goods were handled here for about three years after the end of passenger services. The loco is a BR Type 2 Bo-Bo of 1,250 horsepower, a type first appearing in 1958 with No. D5000.

A Stanier Class 4 2-6-4T No. 42631 has left Wigan Central at 14.00, called at Lower Ince and is now coming to a stop at Hindley South with a train for Manchester Central. It is running as a Pacific Tank, i.e., bunker-first. Apparently, crews were happy with this as the cab gave adequate protection and the loco ran more smoothly in reverse! Beyond the bridge, spurs branch off to west and east. The south to east spur, to Amberswood East Junction on the Whelley line, was busy on summer Saturdays with trains to Blackpool, some from places deep into Midland Railway territory such as Leicester and Nottingham. Picture dated 1 July 1964.

It's now Sunday 1 November 1964 and the final curtain for the ex-GCR line into Wigan. Fortunately, Springs Branch has turned out Standard Class 4 4-6-0 No. 75057 to work one of the last trains to Manchester Central. No. 75057 is passing through Bickershaw & Abram Station, which appears to be closed on Sundays. The facilities here are very basic and the illumination is by oil lamps only, not even upgraded to gas! The cessation date of the passenger service from Wigan Central to Glazebrook was officially recorded as 2 November 1964.

By the end of 1963 the original number of 38 Duchess Pacifics had been reduced to 22 and another three had gone by the date of this picture, 4 August 1964. No. 46243 *City of Lancaster*, working an Edge Hill—Carlisle freight, has stopped for a crew change just beyond Ince Moss Junction and will join the main line at Springs Branch, about a quarter of a mile ahead. The presence of WD 2-8-0 No. 90399 alongside invites comparison of 8P and 8F motive power, No. 46243 having a much larger boiler and firebox, therefore greater potential power output. For this class of freight work, which was usually within the capacity of a Black 5, the Duchesses were not economical to operate, so in the absence of passenger work which would require their power output, all were withdrawn by the end of September – regardless of their actual condition.

2954

By 2 February 1968 diesel incursion is really gaining momentum and English Electric Type 4 No. D202 is working a lengthy coal train from Bickershaw Collieries. Platt Bridge Junction signal box is visible in the distance as it, very cautiously, approaches Firtree House Junction where it will join the Whelley line and pass over the West Coast Main Line. The gradient down to Ince Moss has reportedly steepened to 1 in 45 by this time due to mining subsidence and the virtually straight road through the junction will be kept clear in case No. D202 loses control of its train. Will some brakes be pinned down as there is no brake tender attached to the loco?

Opposite: Much of the shunting activity at Ince Moss is centred on the nearby refuse sidings. On 4 November 1966 Stanier Mogul No. 42954 finds itself in a very precarious-looking position as the wagons are unloaded. Is that debris from a railway building down there? Could there be some interesting steam-age artefacts buried here?

No. 42954 is destined to be the last Stanier Mogul in service, withdrawn in February 1967, just beating the now preserved No. 42968, which had gone in December 1966.

It's a wintry scene in Platt Bridge on 28 December 1967. Springs Branch shed had ceased to operate steam on the 4th of that month but there was still steam activity in the area. In early 1968 several South Lancashire sheds, including Speke, Edge Hill, Newton Heath and Bolton, were still operating steam, likewise Lostock Hall, Rose Grove and Carnforth further north. Their locos, mainly Black 5s or 8Fs were even seen on Springs Branch shed for coaling and watering well into 1968. In this picture an 8F, probably No. 48720 from Bolton, banked by another 8F, has come from Ince Moss, taken the Whelley Line at Firtree House Junction and is heading towards Amberswood West Junction. The crew will not like running tender-first on a very cold day but the train will reverse at De Trafford Junction and, now running forwards, 48720 will become the banker as they join the ex-LYR line at Hindley No. 2 signal box.

A couple of hundred yards from the previous location on the same day, 28 December 1967, an 8F, hiding its identity behind clouds of steam, is having great difficulty lifting its long train of empty 16-ton mineral wagons past Platt Bridge Junction. It has left the main line at Springs Branch, Manchester Junction, and passed Cromptons Sidings signal box before getting into difficulties on the climb to Platt Bridge. However, it keeps moving and the train will be delivered, if a little late, to Abram North, the location of the exchange sidings for Bickershaw Collieries.

On Sunday 28 March 1965 some passengers on this Glasgow to Birmingham train, diverted off the main line at Springs Branch, Manchester Junction, may appreciate the subsequent sight-seeing trip through the Manchester area. The loco is one of the by then ubiquitous English Electric Type 4s, No. D221 named *Ivernia*. At Bickershaw Junction, the branch off to the colliery complex can be seen in the foreground. The signal box has a very squat appearance due to the effect of mining subsidence in this area. It is, in fact, of the normal height, the track having been progressively raised to counteract subsidence over many years.

Opposite: A trip down the branch from Bickershaw Junction now, for a reminder that steam was still to be seen in the area many years after its demise on the main line. At Bickershaw Collieries, Austerity 0-6-0ST, named *Respite* and built by Hunslet in Leeds in 1950, Works No. 3696, is hard at work on 3 November 1975. This loco had been seen at Astley Green on 26 February 1968 and possibly moved to Bickershaw after closure of that colliery. It has been fitted, along with many other NCB locos, with the Giesel Ejector exhaust system in an attempt to increase steaming capacity with poor quality coal.

An immaculate Ivatt Mogul basks in the evening sunshine at Springs Branch on 19 May 1966. Emerging from Swindon Works in January 1953, No. 46517 still carries the green livery applied by Swindon to the last 25 of these LMS-designed locos, numbered 46503—46527. All 25 were initially allocated to the Western Region, most to Oswestry, No. 46517 moving to the London Midland Region when about 10 years old.

There has been a depot on or very near this site since the 1840s and new facilities for the stabling and maintenance of modern electric traction units have recently come into use.

Opposite: Almost a year later, 17 September 1976, another Austerity or J94 0-6-0ST is photographed at Bickershaw. It is one of the older examples, built by Robert Stephenson & Hawthorn in 1944, Works No. 7135 and named *Gwyneth*, probably because it spent at least some of its earlier life in Wales, having been seen at Gresford Colliery on 12 August 1971. To complete the steam scene at Bickershaw, it is worth mentioning that Shafts 1 and 3 had steam winding engines until 1977 and eight Lancashire Boilers were still in use in 1975. Steam shunting was seen in 1983, the 'super pit' eventually closing on 13 March 1992.

At Springs Branch again, on 12 July 1964, a BR Standard Class 4 4-6-0 No. 75041 is undergoing maintenance work on its motion, probably the relatively simple task of renewing the brasses. Parts on the floor include a connecting rod. Its refitting will be a heavy lift for at least two men but it is a much cleaner environment than a smokebox and it is well lit.

No. 75041 is an Springs Branch (8F) engine at this time, and was withdrawn from Carnforth in February 1968 after a spell at Skipton. Only seven Standards survived until The End—five 75XXXs, plus 73069 and 70013.

Opposite: Springs Branch had been coded 10A until February 1958, when it was apparently downgraded to 8F. As the chief shed of a wide area, it carried out light repairs on a great number of locomotives, work which continued until closure to steam, late in 1967.

On 27 February 1966 the boiler and smokebox of an 8F are ready for inspection. The smokebox has been cleaned out but inspection and possible repair to leaky tubes, superheater or steam pipes is still a very dirty job.

Springs Branch Black 5 No. 45313 has been involved in an accident near Bickershaw Junction, a collision with another Black 5, and it was the entirely innocent party. It has been pushed into the workshop but was repair ever seriously contemplated? Running light engine tender first, it was waiting for the road at the down starter signal and in the prevailing poor weather conditions, the signalman forgot about it. As there was no track circuitry, a parcels train could be accepted and signals pulled off. No. 45313 moved off and the faster-moving parcels train, hauled by another Black 5, No. 45414, ran into it. Nobody was seriously hurt but the locos suffered almost identical fatal injuries.

The November of 1967 certainly lived up to its reputation as a dull and misty month, especially on Saturday mornings around Springs Branch. On the 4th, Black 5 No. 44761 has been prepared for its day's work while an English Electric Type 4 diesel lurks in the background, a reminder that the takeover will soon be completed. In the distance, looking through the mist, the emerging sun reflects off the frost-covered roof of the No. 1 signal box and the loaded coal wagons may well satisfy demand until the end of steam.

A flashback in time now to 30 June 1960 and one of my earliest pictures, taken from a favourite spot, the lineside near Taylor's Lane bridge. Super D (LNWR G2) No. 49451, running light engine, is heading back to shed from Bamfurlong sorting sidings on the freight lines. At this point these lines are on the eastern side of the main lines, and, to avoid conflicting movements, pass under these four tracks to access the marshalling yard on the western side.

No. 49451 is very clean and may well have had a recent overhaul at Crewe, as it survived until December 1962. On 22 September 1962 it must have been still in good condition as it toured the Preston area on that section of the Mid-Lancs Rail Tour.

Previous spread left: On the same morning, Saturday 4 November 1967, an unidentified 8F reverses off shed, having been given priority over a Black 5 on the left. The crews, who will have to take extra care in these conditions, exchange greetings as the 8F disappears into the mist. At this late stage, it seemed that Springs Branch was relying on Black 5s or 8Fs to work all its rosters, although Nos. 76075, 76081 and the now-preserved 76077 were still there, maybe either withdrawn or stored.

Right: Moving on to Saturday 2 December 1967, and it really is the last chance to see Springs Branch steam in action as Sunday is likely to be a much quieter day, followed by closure on Monday 4th. After cycling a couple of miles in the seemingly inevitable freezing fog, conditions for photography are rather challenging but hopefully worth the effort.

The light on the left is still on and the sun is beginning to penetrate the gloom as an unidentified 8F moves off shed. It's too cold to be bothered taking notes but this loco may be off to new home, along with a few other Black 5s and 8Fs which were in decent condition and could soldier on into 1968.

Only two hardy enthusiasts observe the last rites from Taylor's Lane bridge.

This is the view from Taylor's Lane bridge on 3 November 1966 as Kingmoor Black 5 No. 45135 heads south on a fitted freight. Familiar 1960s sights are the two train spotters on the lineside and the 'bobby's' car parked behind the No. 1 signal box. The Springs Branch North Sidings box is also visible in the distance but the main line No. 2 box is hidden by the steam. The complexity of Manchester Junction is well illustrated, requiring six diamond crossings, a track formation now avoided as much as possible by Network Rail. There are still six roads at this point, all, including the goods lines, electrified and a very simple track layout suffices to give access to the depot.

Back to the lineside now to see rebuilt Patriot No. 45526 *Morecambe and Heysham* pass by on an Oxley—Carlisle freight on 24 July 1964. No. 2 box has not yet pulled off its distant signal, maybe to make sure the train stops to allow a relief guard, waiting on the track, to get on board. No. 45526 is a Carlisle Upperby loco at this time and looks in good condition, but it was nevertheless withdrawn by the end of October 1964.

In July 1964 virtually all the named locomotives still carried their nameplates. If memory serves correctly, the vast majority were removed in early autumn of that year.

The whole class of 55 Britannia Pacifics was still extant in April 1965, all allocated to the London Midland Region at this time and therefore a common sight passing through Wigan. Nevertheless, this is a very fortuitous meeting under Taylor's Lane bridge. Heading south on a freight train is No. 70028, formerly named *Royal Star,* meeting No. 70023, formerly named *Venus,* on a Euston—Windermere train, formerly the 'Lakes Express'.

Firtree House Junction straddles the bridge in the background, where the Whelley line meets the spur from Platt Bridge Junction, the signal box being just out of the picture on the right. The date is 1 April 1965.

On 24 July 1964, another look at this favourite location. Rebuilt Patriot No. 45530 *Sir Frank Ree* is heading a northbound parcels train and cautiously passing the No. 1 box. No. 2 box, about a quarter of a mile ahead, has not pulled off the distant signal and the driver's intense concentration is evident as he no doubt hopes to get a clear road ahead. No. 45530 was the last Patriot to be withdrawn, from Carlisle Kingmoor in December 1965. A pair of Black 5s involved in maintenance work on the freight lines add interest to this busy scene.

Springs Branch No. 1 signal box, built by the LNWR, had 80 levers and closed on 1 October 1972 when electrification and resignalling work was completed on this section of the West Coast Main Line.

By this time, 2 February 1968, Springs Branch is no longer operating its own locos but steam activity continues in the area. An 8F, No. 48348, from Rose Grove, Burnley, is taking water on the up fast line near the No. 2 signal box. It will shortly set off to deliver a train of coal empties to Bickershaw Collieries as another 8F, No. 48124, an Edge Hill loco, heads north on a coal train from Bickershaw. The No. 2 box dates only from 1933, an LMS replacement for the original LNWR cabin with 75 levers and, as No. 1, closing on 1 October 1972.

Is there time to dash round to Taylor's Lane on the bike to get an action shot of 48348?

Not quite: the approach shot, taken very hurriedly, is not a complete success and the going-away picture proves to be the more interesting. The fireman must be quite happy with his preparations for the steep climb to Platt Bridge Junction as he leans out of the cab for a breath of the cold morning air. The small Cromptons Sidings signal box, which closed on 20 February 1972, was very busy in steam days, controlling both through lines and access to the shed. The CWS Glass Works, visible in the background, was mainly engaged in making containers for the various Co-op products. Cromptons Sidings, once part of the complex web of industrial lines in the Wigan area, diverged on the extreme left, but had been lifted long before this date, 2 February 1968.

Opposite: The scene is now Wigan North Western Station on a very dull, damp and misty 25 November 1967. The quite spectacular passage of Rose Grove 8F No. 48423 on a coal train from Bickershaw does not appear to excite the handful of enthusiasts who are anticipating a more interesting event. No. 48423 looks well prepared for the climb to Coppull Summit, which begins a short distance ahead with almost two miles at 1 in 104 to Boars Head Junction. Note the uneven surface of the flagged platform, typical of many stations in steam days but unlikely to meet present day health and safety concerns.

48423

The keenly anticipated event on 25 November is the arrival of A4 Pacific *Bittern* at Wigan for a water stop. Manchester Rail Travel Society organised the 'Lancashire and Yorkshire Rambler', an extensive tour starting from Leeds City. The train has, however, has become 'The Mancunian' on arrival at Wigan! No. 60019 has come via Hellifield and Carnforth and will continue via Eccles, Manchester Piccadilly, Guide Bridge, Stockport, Miles Platting, Manchester Victoria, Clifton, Bury, Heywood and Mirfield to return to Leeds City. This could not be repeated today as some sections of the route have gone, e.g. Clifton to Bury.

The signalmen at Nos. 1 and 2 boxes will be aware that the West Coast Main Line is blocked by mass trespassing! A lenient view of such behaviour was often taken at this time and there is no sign of any intervention by staff or police.

Britannia Pacific No. 70009, formerly named *Alfred the Great,* eases the 13.46 Barrow—Euston out of Wigan North Western on 29 June 1966. It's a beautiful sunny day, so what can possibly go wrong? No. 70009 produces a great column of black smoke and puts itself in the shade! The fireman has obviously been very busy even though it's an easy run to Warrington. Maybe he is planning to sit down and have a bite to eat?

No. 1 signal box, one of three ARP boxes built during the Second World War, controls the LYR lines on the left as well as the main line. It is actually two separate boxes with an internal dividing wall. Resignalling along with electrification resulted in the closure of all the main line boxes in the area on 1 October 1972, when the Warrington power box took over.

Moving on now to 21 October 1966 and another look of the 13.46 Barrow—Euston at Wigan. By this time, it was one of the very few steam-hauled passenger trains on this section of the main line and usually hauled by a Carlisle Kingmoor Britannia. No. 70053, formerly named *Moray Firth,* slowly approaches on the falling gradient, which makes it more difficult for the driver to stop in the right place.

This station was opened as Wigan on 31 October 1838 and renamed Wigan North Western on 2 June 1924, the LYR station losing its old company name, and renamed Wigan Wallgate at the same time. The LNWR had enlarged its station between 1888 and 1894 and it then remained largely unaltered until rebuilt in 1971/2 as part of the electrification project. A picture almost identical to this one, apart from the motive power, could have been taken about 70 years earlier!

From Euston, milepost 1 marks the top of Camden Bank. The next noteworthy gradient starts at milepost 194: Boars Head Bank north of Wigan. On 7 September 1966 an unidentified Britannia Pacific is silhouetted against the setting sun as it climbs towards Rylands Sidings on a parcels train. The lower part of the bank had to be built on quite a high embankment to even out the gradient, which, however, still had to be set at a steep 1 in 104 up to Boars Head Junction, near to milepost 196.

Britannias were much in evidence throughout 1966 and there were still 42 in service at the year end.

Further up the bank, on the sunny side of the line between Rylands Sidings and Boars Head, Carnforth Black 5 No. 44894 is making light work of the climb with a fitted freight. It almost appears to be running in mid-gear! The fireman, shielding his eyes from the bright sunshine, poses for the camera.

This is perhaps a surprisingly rural setting not far from the centre of Wigan and remains so today, now cloaked by dense woodland.

This is really light work for Lostock Hall Black 5 No. 45347, heading north at Boars Head Junction early on a July morning in 1967 with a very short parcels train. The branch to Adlington, almost disused by this time, is in the foreground. This latter route was opened on 1 November 1869 and lost its regular passenger service on 4 April 1960, finally closing to goods traffic on 25 May 1971. Passenger trains, diverted off the main line, were seen on this route until its final closure.

20

Opposite: A little later on this July 1967 morning, an alternative view of Boars Head Junction and yet another Black 5. Is this the most useful locomotive ever to run on British railways? No. 45061, one of the older examples, emerging from Vulcan Foundry in December 1934, heads north on a fitted freight and may take it through to Carlisle as it is allocated to Kingmoor at this time. This view shows the tall signals protecting the junction, which can be sighted against the sky rather than a confusing background at a lower level. The main line signal is offset to permit sighting past the signal box for southbound trains, the distants being controlled from Rylands Sidings box about half way down the bank.

Right: It's worth having a close look at the distinctive signal box at Boars Head Junction as a Newton Heath Black 5, No. 45254, comes into view on a southbound freight on the same morning. The high position ensures good sightlines along the main lines and the branch.

Boars Head Station, which closed on 31 January 1949, lay immediately north of the junction with platforms on all four lines, the up main and down branch lines meeting under the cabin. This layout probably dated from the opening of the branch to passengers on 1 December 1869, although there was certainly a station here from 31 October 1838.

The Wigan Avoiding Line (the Whelley Line) joined the main line at Standish Junction just over a mile north of Boars Head and an underpass was provided for northbound trains to avoid conflicting movements with southbound main line traffic. On 15 July 1964 a Blackpool 'stopper' has left Wigan at 16.34, hauled by Black 5 No. 45073, which has shut off steam to cross over to the slow line a short distance ahead.

This short link from Whelley Junction to Standish Junction opened on 5 June 1882 to complete the avoiding line and it looks as if this bridge has been repaired at least twice since then. However, the most recent brickwork has already become thoroughly smoke-blackened by locos working hard to climb the gradient up to the main line, itself rising at 1 in 366.

It appears to require a huge effort from 8F (downgraded from 9F) 2-10-0 No. 92025 to lift a heavy car-carrying train off the Whelley Line up to the down slow line at Standish Junction. The loco, probably to the relief of the crew, is now on an easier gradient and will slowly pick up speed.

No. 92025 is one of 10 9Fs built with a Franco-Crosti boiler but working conventionally by this time, 23 January 1965. A preheat boiler, to heat the feed water, was slung beneath the main boiler, hoping that this would reduce coal consumption. This was not achieved, but the design allowed the preheater to be sealed off and the engine to be worked conventionally. The boiler was, however, smaller than standard, hence the downgrading from 9 to 8F.

This picture revives a remarkable memory of Saturday 17 August 1957, when, from this very spot, I saw a Crosti-boilered 9F on a passenger train when No.92022 from 15A (Wellingborough) came off the Whelley Line on its way to Blackpool.

On 15 July 1964, 9F No. 92161, a Newton Heath loco at this time, passes Standish Junction with a Carlisle—Manchester fitted freight. At present on the slow line, it will shortly join the up fast line to take it through Wigan and leave the main line at Springs Branch Manchester Junction.

The main buildings of Standish Station were in the foreground of this picture on an island platform; closure was on 23 May 1949, after having been opened in late 1838 or sometime in 1839.

Opposite: Fairburn Class 4 2-6-4T No. 42187 is heading the 18.54 Wigan—Preston local through Standish Junction on 15 May 1964. It has been diverted onto the slow line and given a clear road to the north, where the first stop will be Coppull. The crossover starting immediately in front of No. 42187 allows trains coming from Whelley to transfer to the fast line. The northbound platform of the station was on the right of the picture.

Tank engines did not last until the end of steam, but No. 42187 was a comparatively late survivor, withdrawn in May 1967 from Lostock Hall.

STANDISH JUNCTION
42187

Now looking north from the same spot, rebuilt Patriot No. 45531 *Sir Frederick Harrison*, a Carlisle Kingmoor loco, is signalled to take the Whelley Line with a fitted freight. It will re-join the main line at Bamfulong Junction, five miles to the south. No. 45531 looks rather unkempt on 27 July 1964 but still has its nameplate and it did survive until October 1965, the last Patriot No. 45530 going by the end of that year.

There are two other interesting features in this picture. Standish Junction is working to its full capacity, with trains also signalled on the up and down slow lines. The up train could run alongside No. 45531 to take the Wigan line. The down train could be coming from Wigan or Whelley. Finally, the tidiness of the whole area is quite striking, not a blade of grass or a piece of ballast out of place!

Also on 27 July 1964, something unusual turns up. The 8F No. 48223, allocated to Fleetwood at this time, has been pressed into service on a lengthy southbound parcels train. If memory serves correctly, there had been a postal strike not long before this date and a large backlog of mail had to be cleared. The train is coming off the slow line, which shortly crosses the down fast line and is signalled to go down to Wigan rather than Whelley.

Note that the slow line still has the older chaired bullhead rail, but the fast lines have been upgraded to the modern flat-bottomed type, which will probably give a smoother ride.

Finally, at Standish Junction, a one-off event: the appearance of Peppercorn A2 Pacific No. 60528 *Tudor Minstrel*. On 23 April 1966, Altringham Railway Society organised the 'Waverley Special', which ran from Manchester Exchange to Edinburgh via Carlisle and the Waverley route, returning via Newcastle and York. V2s Nos. 60824 and 60836 were involved in the return run with Jubilee No. 45565 on the last leg back to Manchester. No. 60528 is in fine voice as it climbs to Coppull Summit less than two miles ahead, but Shap and the Waverley route will be a much sterner test. Its exertions on this day may have hastened its demise, which was only two months later! Although a completely LNER-designed loco, No. 60528 emerged from Doncaster Works in February 1948 and therefore was never owned by that company. Its name, by the way, has equine rather than musical connotations. Tudor Minstrel had won the 2000 Guineas in 1947, so this was a continuation of an LNER tradition.

Chapter Four South East Lancashire

This ex-LYR saddletank, shunting at Horwich Works on 7 August 1964 is looking rather work-stained. No. 11305 is the oldest locomotive working on BR at this time, built in 1877 to a Barton-Wright design as a tender locomotive and rebuilt as a saddletank in 1891 after Aspinall had become Chief Mechanical Engineer. By 1964, it is aged 87. In 1954 there were six of these locos at the works, five still carrying their LMS numbers, Crewe Works also having three in BR days. No. 11456 was purchased by a colliery in 1937 and is now preserved. No. 11305 was, however, withdrawn in September 1964, only a month or so after this photograph was taken, and the class was finally extinct on BR.

Another Horwich Works shunter, also withdrawn in September 1964, is Fowler Dock Tank No. 47165 which has strayed out of the works area and across the running lines leading to Horwich Station. The last two survivors of this small class of only 10 engines were employed at Horwich until withdrawn in September 1964, the other one being No. 47164.

Horwich turned out its first locomotive, Radial Tank No. 1008, now in the NRM, in August 1889. The last standard gauge locomotive, the 1,830th was BR Standard Class 4 2-6-0 No. 76099, emerging on 27 November 1957. The last steam locomotive overhauled was 8F No. 48756, which left the works on 6 May 1964. New construction turned to 350hp diesel shunters from August 1958 and 169 diesels had been built by the end of 1962, the last one numbered D4157.

Opposite: Before leaving the Horwich area, a reminder that industrial steam was also in sharp decline in the 1960s. On 14 September 1967 this 20-year-old Andrew Barclay lies out of use at the Cooke & Nuttall paper mill near Blackrod. It still has its maker's plate, works No. 2230 1947, and there has been some effort to protect it against the elements but nevertheless it's a sad sight. The takeover by road transport is also evident in the photograph. Rivington Pike, a well-known local landmark, dominates the background.

Bolton West on 9 June 1967 and a picture illustrating the complexity of the junction in steam days. There are no less than 10 diamond crossings in the picture. Black 5 No. 45304 is passing over four in quick succession to go through to Platform 1. The other six are necessary to connect all four roads through the centre of the station to the Blackburn line coming in on the right. Out of sight behind the signal box there is a chord allowing trains to avoid the station, which requires two more junctions. All this is controlled by Bolton West signal box, which was the first in Britain to use an electro-pneumatic system to control points and signals on a passenger line.

Black 5 No. 44709 takes the through road at Bolton West with a freight from the north, on 15 May 1968. The distinctive footbridge certainly dates from LYR days, probably from the years 1900 to 1904 when the station was rebuilt and the electro-pneumatic signalling system installed. Bolton West box had 83 small levers at 2½ inch centres on a frame only 18 feet long. There were 44 to work signals and 30 to work points, leaving nine spare. The system came into use on 27 September 1903. A traditional mechanical frame would have been at least 56 feet long to perform the same functions.

BRITISH RAILWAYS
44709

On a dull and misty September morning in 1966 at Bolton the through-road signals are pulled off for the 07.25 Blackpool—Manchester express and a suitable camera position is chosen. However, the appearance of Black 5 No. 45275 on the 07.45 Blackburn—Manchester 'stopper' on a train that has recently been worked by a DMU is a complete surprise. It transpired later that this train had reverted to steam haulage for a few weeks around this time and, at least on this occasion, by a Rose Grove loco. Blackburn's Lower Darwen shed (10H) had closed in February 1966, so this was probably normal practice until reversion to a DMU.

Opposite: When No. 44709 passed Bolton West, the east box had not pulled off the distant so it looks as if the Black 5 will be checked about 200 yards ahead. Due to the curvature of the road, the fireman is in a better position than the driver to see the signals and concentrates on the road ahead.

No. 44709 was one of comparatively few locos that spent almost their entire lives at one shed. Built in October 1948 at Horwich, it went to Carnforth in January 1949 and stayed there until The End, in August 1968.

A DMU forming the 17.37 to Wigan is about to leave Platform 4 at Bolton on the 9 June 1967. By this time there was little or no steam on local passenger trains in the area and today even DMUs are but a memory. This picture attempts to record the LYR lower-quadrant signals suspended from above in a very dark spot, one of them pulled off for the departure of the 17.37. This scene, apart from the presence of 1960s motive power, will have changed very little since the rebuilding of the station was completed in 1904.

The through roads have gone today and consequently the junction at Bolton West has been greatly simplified. A bus station now stands in the area once occupied by the signal box and the avoiding line. Another recent development is the electrification of the Manchester—Preston route.

This is another almost purely LYR scene, one recorded by chance at Bolton on 15 May 1968. On arrival at the barrier the sound of an approaching locomotive is heard, the camera hurriedly set up and Black 5 No. 45073 is snapped passing through Platform 1 with a brake van in tow. The eight trolleys on the platform are an indication of the importance of parcels traffic. Note the unattended packages on the farthest trolley – not a cause for concern in 1968!

Most of the station buildings at Bolton have been retained, with the roof, but the original entrance and the fine LYR staircase seen here have been demolished.

A few minutes later on 15 May 1968, No. 45073 reappears without the brake van and moves alongside Platform 1. The goods yard appears to be quite busy and even well equipped for night working. The 'mechanical horses' were still a fairly common sight at this time. The impressive warehouse, still proudly displaying the name of its former owner, dominates the scene and certainly dwarfs the Black 5. This building, of considerable architectural merit, was demolished some years ago and the site is now occupied by modern commercial buildings, i.e. large metal boxes.

Now for something completely different: an electrified industrial railway. The coal-burning Kearsley Power Station operated a fleet of four Bo-Bo electric locomotives, built by Thompson-Houston. The power station was situated on the northern side of the Bolton to Manchester line, but at a much lower level. The connection with BR passed beneath the main line and curved very sharply on a steep gradient to gain access to the exchange sidings. One of the electric locos is seen climbing this gradient with no apparent effort on a train of empty 16-ton mineral wagons. This incline would probably have been impossible to work with steam. The date is 23 March 1967.

To give access to the network of colliery railways in the area, the sidings at Kearsley were connected to exchange sidings at Linnyshaw Moss in 1878 by Kearsley No. 1 Branch. So, on the same day, 23 March 1967, it only takes a few minutes on the bike to explore that area. Luckily, an industrial locomotive of unusual interest soon appears, running light engine to pick up its next load.

Sir Robert is one of five North Staffordshire Railway 0-6-2Ts purchased from the LMS in 1937. By March 1967 it had seen 46 years' service since it emerged from Stoke Works in 1921. It was the last of the five still at work and withdrawal was later in 1967.

By the start of 1968, main line steam was obviously in terminal decline – likewise on industrial lines, but here the situation was not quite as critical. There is still some spectacular action, matching anything seen or heard on the main line, at Astley Green Colliery on 26 February 1968. Austerity 0-6-0ST *Harry* is making an all-out effort to lift a mixed rake of coal wagons out of the colliery yard. *Harry* is one of the older Austerities, built by Hudswell-Clarke in 1944, Works No. 1776. The Hunslet Engine Company designed these locos to the specification of Riddles for the Ministry of Supply and several hundred were built between 1943 and 1946. The LNER purchased 75 of these powerful locos (T.E. 23,870 lbs) after the Second World War. Later, as Class J94, they were numbered 68006—68080 and given a 4F power classification.

Before leaving the Astley Green area, a look at steam in the landscape created by coal mining: the smoke from another J94 saddletank, *Allen,* also built by Hudswell-Clarke in 1944, Works No.1777, dominates the wasteland created by the dumping of spoil since the colliery was first sunk in 1908. The line on the right descends to Chat Moss to connect with the Liverpool and Manchester Railway at Astley and much of the tunnelling from the pithead lies beneath it.

The colliery closed in 1970 and nature soon started to reclaim the area. The picture also dates from 26 February 1968.

BR Standard 5MT 4-6-0 No. 73156 is one of many locos built in the 1950s that had a very short working life. Emerging from Doncaster Works in December 1956, it was withdrawn in November 1967. It is seen here about to take the Bolton line at Bury Knowsley Street Station on 21 April 1967. The huge Lancashire and Yorkshire Railway Cotton Warehouse dominates the eastern end of the station, but it has probably outlived its original function by this time.

The warehouse and station are now long-gone and Metrolink trams now pass through this location on their way to the town centre. The East Lancashire Railway now operates a single line to Heywood, steep gradients being needed to bridge the tram lines, leaving no trace of Knowsley Street Station. Continuing on a happier note, No. 73156 was saved for preservation and is running on the Great Central Railway at the time of writing.

There is some unconventional steam activity at the paper mill of Yates, Duxbury & Son at Heap Bridge near Bury in February 1968. It seems that paper was recycled in 1968, but some of the handling facilities were rather rudimentary! Peckett 0-6-0ST *May* Works No. 1370, built in 1915, has apparently dropped a bale of waste paper off its buffer beam onto the track and must now assist with its retrieval. The bale was eventually delivered to the factory more or less intact!

An 8F, No. 48090, is about to pass through Manchester Victoria Station, running light engine back to its then home shed, Newton Heath, on 6 June 1967. The 'light' engine and tender does, in fact, weigh 125 tons, which must shortly be lifted up the 1 in 47 gradient of Miles Platting Bank, so the fireman has obviously prepared for this. The roof of Exchange Station, which is in Salford, is visible on the right and No. 48090 is crossing the River Irwell, which forms the boundary between Manchester and Salford. Its tender may still be in Salford!

The building in the left foreground is of LYR origin and this, with everything else relating to the railway in this picture, has gone. There is hardly any trace of Exchange Station and only four very busy through platforms plus two bays at Victoria.

On 22 October 1966 a tour organised by Liverpool University Public Transport Society ran a now unrepeatable tour from Liverpool, using two long-gone stations. Starting at Riverside and finishing at Central, four locomotives were used: 2-6-4T No. 42233 to Manchester, assisted by Black 5 No. 45015 to Edge Hill and finishing with Crab No. 42942; Britannia Pacific No. 70004, formerly named *William Shakespeare,* took over at Manchester for the run to Birkenhead, where the Crab was waiting for the final leg. In those days rail tours were certainly good fun; you could even lean out of windows and take photographs! This opportunity was taken after No. 70004 had successfully climbed Miles Platting Bank and is rounding the sharp curve just beyond the station.

Chapter Five

Yorkshire and the North East

Overleaf: 9F 2-10-0 No. 92233 is passing through Long Preston Station with one of the Long Meg—Widnes anhydrite trains on 15 August 1966. Note that there are still some sleepers lying around on the right where sidings have been lifted, likewise on the down side. The signal box is out of use and awaiting demolition as all the signals and points have been removed.

No. 92233 is one of 262 steam locomotives built in BR days that had a working life of less than 10 years, leaving Crewe Works in August 1958 and withdrawn from Speke Junction on 2 February 1968. A Carlisle Kingmoor loco in August 1966, it did, unlike many others, manage to survive the closure of that shed at the end of 1967. *Photo by Joan Heyes*

On the same day, 15 August 1966, Holbeck Jubilee 4-6-0 No. 45697 *Achilles* also passes through Long Preston on a southbound freight. The station buildings date back to Midland days but were unfortunately replaced by 'bus shelters' long ago. There is also a glimpse of some typical Midland Railway fencing and the redundant signal box. Observant passengers may, however, notice a Midland Railway milepost still embedded in the up platform, 232½ miles (from St. Pancras by their old route).There were nine surviving Jubilees at this time, four of them at Holbeck: Nos. 45562, 45593, 45675 and 45697.

Moving on now to a location of some historical importance about a quarter of a mile south of the present Hellifield Station. Haw Grove Crossing was the site of the first Hellifield Station, a location closer to the old village centre than the present station. By 1 June 1880 the LYR had completed their extension from Chatburn to Hellifield and the present station opened on this date. The fine-looking house, probably built for the Station Master, was demolished many years ago and all traces of the station have disappeared.

Holbeck 8F No. 48104 heads a northbound freight on a very gloomy 17 May 1967. Fitted with a small snowplough, maybe with the Carlisle route in mind, it was nevertheless withdrawn a couple of months later.

On the same day, 17 May 1967, here is a sequence of three pictures recording steam activity at Skipton featuring one of the last four Jubilees to operate from Holbeck, No. 45562 *Alberta.*

This station, opened in April 1876, was a replacement for the original, which lay a short distance to the south. As No. 45562, checked by adverse signals, crawls through Platform 2, the Midland Railway atmosphere can be appreciated – something that is still evident in this century. The DMU on the left may be waiting to depart on a train to Colne and beyond, as this line survived until 1970.

Opposite: The signals controlled by Skipton Station South box remain at danger as the driver slowly inches No. 45562 forward. The nameplate: is it the genuine article or a replica? Nameplates had generally disappeared by this time. It seems to be an Ivatt Mogul No. 43105 causing the delay, as it reverses a short freight across the lines ahead.

The first Skipton Station, the site now occupied by a supermarket, would have just about got into this picture behind No. 43105.

45562

No. 43105 has now gained access to the branch north of the station and is heading off towards Grassington as No. 45562 finally comes to a stop. The splitting distants are controlled by the box at Skipton South Junction to give advance warning of the route ahead, main line or loop. Note the Midland water column at the platform end, but does a tender locomotive have to overrun the signal to use it?

No. 43105 had spent 13 years on the Eastern Region before its transfer to Carnforth in October 1964. On this day, 17 May 1967, it was very near the end of its life, withdrawn by the end of the month. No. 45562 was officially withdrawn in November 1967, the last Jubilee to operate on the main line before the preservation era.

On 1 October 1967 the branch platform at Skipton was still accessible even though services to Ilkley had ceased in 1965. The preserved Gresley A4 Pacific No. 4498 *Sir Nigel Gresley* is seen from that high vantage point, coasting into Platform 3 for a water stop. *Sir Nigel* is taking the 'Splendour of Steam Rail Tour' from Peterborough to Carlisle, resplendent in LNER blue livery and number carried when it emerged from 'The Plant' at Doncaster in November 1937. Its Kylchap blastpipe and double chimney has been retained even though it was only fitted in January 1958 when the loco was, of course, in BR green livery. GWR Castle No. 7029 *Clun Castle* worked the return run as far as Engine Shed Junction, Leeds. Will the youngsters on the platform remember this notable event?

man gets real pleasure from PLAYER'S

The Eastern Region considered the Deltics to be worthy successors to their large fleet of Pacifics and ordered 22 examples. On 8 July 1966, D9013 *The Black Watch* is leaving York with the down 'Heart of Midlothian', the two Napier Deltic engines producing the familiar exhaust pattern and, unfortunately, leaving behind the all-pervading smell of diesel fumes.

Note the two young train spotters sitting on a trolley, a familiar sight in this bygone era.

Opposite: Watering facilities were retained right up to the end of steam on most routes, making the planning of rail tours much easier in this respect than it is today. No. 4498's water stop at Skipton, seen from beneath the water tower, results in the familiar unsupervised mass trespassing of the period.

The elegant lines of the A4 Pacific are shown to advantage here. Also note the practicality of the design, the running board allowing easy access to oil and sand boxes through small hatches in the casing.

Some readers may remember the then-familiar advertisement for Player's cigarettes on the bridge in the background, such large posters being part of the railway environment in steam days.

The RCTS, West Riding Branch, organised 'The Blyth and Tyne Rail Tour', to run on 19 September 1965, the very complex route involving many now-closed lines. One example is the line from Harrogate to Northallerton via Ripon. A4 Pacific No. 60004 *William Whitelaw* started the tour at Leeds City, has come through Harrogate and is seen here joining the East Coast Main Line just south of Northallerton Station. It will, however, now head eastwards to Eaglescliffe, where No. D6769 will take over for the run to Darlington North Road, leaving No. 60004 to run light engine to Darlington.

A highlight of the tour is a visit to the Darlington North Road Works of the former North Eastern Railway, where Class Q6 0-8-0 No. 63395 is undergoing repair at its birthplace. Emerging from the works in December 1918, it is destined to be one of three Q6s to survive until the end of steam in the north east in September 1967, the other two being 63344 and 63387. This trio, with five J27s, were the only pre-grouping locos active on BR by this time. Nos. 63395 and 65894 have been preserved.

Darlington North Road Works was established in 1863 by the Stockton and Darlington Railway. Between 1962 and 1966 BR reorganised its workshops and Darlington was run down and finally closed in 1966.

On 10 October 1825 passengers on a train from Stockton were, reportedly, able to alight in the vicinity of North Road, Darlington. The present North Road Station was, however, opened much later, on 1 April 1842 and is now a Grade-2 listed building. No. 60004 is now leaving North Road for Newcastle on a route now closed, via Bishop Auckland and Durham. The train, hauled by Ivatt 2-6-0 No. 43057 then toured various lines north of the Tyne, taking in Morpeth and Blaydon before returning to Pelaw. Here, the A4 then took over again for the run back to Leeds via Washington, Stockton and Eaglescliffe.

J27 No. 65833 was perhaps highly regarded by the staff at Sunderland shed as they had retained it at least since nationalisation. Heading south along the main line from Sunderland on 11 July 1966 with a pick-up freight at Ryhope Grange Junction, it is signalled into a loop or siding for a shunting movement. The impressive signal gantry controls the southbound main line and the four roads on the right to and from the docks.

By July 1966, No. 65833 was just over 57 years old, but by the time of my next visit, a year later, it was gone.

On the same day, 11 July 1966, there is time for a look at Pontop Crossing. Q6s were unfortunately proving to be somewhat camera shy but eventually No. 63413 approaches with just a brake van in tow and clatters over the crossing, heading towards its home base at Tyne Dock. A total of 120 Q6s were built, the first 70 at Darlington from February 1913, the last 50 by Armstrong Whitworth between November 1919 and March 1921. No. 63413 had a lifespan of 47 years from early 1920 to early 1967.

Opposite: A short time later there is some far more spectacular action at Pontop Crossing when 9F No. 92098 approaches with an iron ore train for the steelworks at Consett. It will have had banking assistance out of Tyne Dock and will also need some further help before reaching Consett.

Tyne Dock acquired 10 9Fs in the mid-1950s for this arduous work. Ten years later withdrawals began and the only survivor for a short time was No. 92065, which went to Wakefield in November 1966.

92098

65855

The River Blyth separates the South and North Blyth sheds, and the nearest bridge is about a mile upstream so it's easier to take the ferry. The North shed is found to be far more substantial than the South, with a pair of J27s and at least one K1 2-6-0 in the roundhouse. On the right, No. 65813 appears to be having a day off, while No.65804, with a full head of steam, looks very impatient to leave.

Steam was active here right up to September 1967.

Opposite: Now we venture north of the Tyne for a look at the Blyth sheds and their J27s on 7 July 1966. At South Blyth the facilities are, to say the least, basic. The hinged cover at the base of the smokebox is open, apparently to allow ash to be simply dropped on the ground beneath. A shovel and wheelbarrow will be needed to tidy up later.

No. 65855 looks quite dishevelled in July 1966, but it is one of the pre-grouping locos that ran until September 1967, when the North Eastern Region eliminated steam. The other J27 survivors were Nos. 65811, 65879, 65882 and the preserved No. 65894. The last day of regular steam working at South Blyth was 26 May 1967, when J27s Nos. 65789 and 65795 were active.

Chapter Six Northern Rail Rover 29 June—5 July 1967

It's soon time to leave on the 06.46 to Mirfield, which leaves on time in pouring rain. There is no sign of steam at Huddersfield or Mirfield, where the sheds have been closed. However, a photograph of some historical interest is taken at Mirfield when an English Electric Type 4 No. D352 passes through on a west-bound coal train.

In 1932 the LMS installed 'Speed Signalling' along the three-mile stretch of line between Heaton Lodge and Thornhill Junctions. It involved the use of red, yellow and green lights, which could indicate stop or a safe speed by using various combinations of those colours. The Cleckheaton Branch diverges to the left in the distance and this signalling system, as can be seen, becomes quite complicated at junctions. Nevertheless, it continued in use until May 1970, when the whole area was resignalled.

Opposite: It's unwise to rely on Wigan Corporation buses at five o'clock in the morning, so the Rail Rover week begins on Thursday 29 June 1967, at 05.00 with a one-and-a-half-mile walk to Wigan North Western Station, On arrival at about 05.30, the Liverpool portion of a train from Glasgow is leaving behind 'Peak' No. D165 as Standard 5MT No.73035 waits in the bay to pick up the Manchester portion, due to depart at 05.45. Departure is, in fact, two minutes early and after a very sedate run to Springs Branch and a very slow climb up to Platt Bridge, the arrival at Manchester Exchange is, surprisingly, on time. It is heartening to see at least six steam locos around Exchange and Victoria: Nos. 73071, 73140, 48504, 45307, 45271 and 45411 are noted.

Under very threatening skies the 08.28 train to Wakefield Kirkgate is boarded where the immediate objective is to check if the shed is still operating steam. A pair of 9Fs, coupled together running light, are noted at Healey Mills but hopes of seeing live steam at Wakefield are dashed.

This forlorn line of dead and condemned locomotives is headed by 2-6-4T No. 42149, followed by WD No. 90650 and Jubilee No. 45647, formerly named *Sturdee*. Further down are three 9Fs, including the former Tyne Dock loco No. 92065.

There are 50 lifeless locomotives on shed: nine 9Fs, 18 WDs, 10 2-6-4Ts, five 8Fs, three Black 5s, three Ivatt 43XXXs, one Jubilee and one B1.

Feeling somewhat depressed, it seems like a long walk back to the Westgate Station on the old GNR line to catch the 10.10 to Leeds City. This arrives on time behind Deltic No. D9012 *Crepello*. The identity of the diesel heading south on a freight is missed as this picture is taken. After a signal check near Holbeck, the arrival at Leeds is two minutes late.

Only one live steam picture has been taken so far but hopes are high for a change in fortune.

Even the weather is now fine, sunny and breezy for the short walk to Holbeck. In the roundhouse a 9F dwarfs all the other locos but it seems that the turntable was probably designed to take the largest Pacifics, about the same length as a 9F. No. 92002 emerged from Crewe in January 1954 and acquired a double chimney in November 1960 when it was on the Western Region. A Birkenhead loco at this time, it may well have brought a train of oil tanks from Ellesmere Port into the Leeds area.

Starting with No. 92183, all the later 9Fs were built with double chimneys and Nos. 92000, 92001, 92002, 92005 and 92006 modified as such in 1960.

Opposite: This optimism is justified as Fairburn Class 4 2-6-4T No. 42689 appears, coupled to Type 2 Bo-Bo diesel No. D5175 to work the 10.38 to Bradford Exchange. Luckily the vestibule window immediately behind No. 42689 is vacant, allowing this shot of the pair leaving Leeds City to be taken. The gradients on this route are severe, as steep as 1 in 50 in some places and the sound of both steam and diesel locomotives working hard at close quarters is a new and memorable experience. The return from Bradford is at 11.55 and the arrival back at Leeds two minutes early.

Other occupants of the roundhouse are Fairburn Class 4 2-6-4T No. 42152 and Black 5 No. 44852, not forgetting the group of schoolboys who are busy collecting numbers. No. 44852 will be withdrawn from Holbeck on closure at the end of September. No. 42152 will shortly be transferred to Low Moor but will not escape withdrawal around the same time. On 1 October 1967, however, the tank will be involved in the last use of steam between Leeds and Bradford.

Holbeck seems quite determined to keep its Jubilees running for as long as possible. No. 45697 *Achilles* appears to have a problem with its middle cylinder but it is being repaired although, inevitably, very near the end of its life, which was just two months later. On the right, No. 45593 *Kolhapur* has been lit up although diary notes say 'wheels very rusty', so it may not have run for some time. Its withdrawal for preservation was in October 1967. The third surviving Jubilee, No. 45562 *Alberta,* is active at this time and will be withdrawn in November.

A break from photography has been planned so it's time to get back to the station and board the 14.30 to Carlisle for a sight-seeing trip over this unfamiliar route. The departure is one minute late behind 'Peak' No. D32 and the arrival bang on time in glorious sunshine. Ivatt Mogul No. 43121 is noted as station pilot before setting off on the long walk to Kingmoor.

The low evening sun is penetrating the gloom at the north end of the shed to create some highlights along this line of locos. The 8F No. 48510 is nearest the camera and with Ivatt 2-6-0s Nos. 43139 and 43120 beyond – all in steam.

My diary notes comment on the 'brilliant sunshine until after 21.00'. The low late evening sunshine is certainly producing some superb reflections off 9F No. 92114 and Britannia Pacific No. 70049, formerly *Moray Firth*. Both appear prepared for action although the 9F has not much life ahead, withdrawn within a month. All the remaining Britannias, except No. 70013, will be withdrawn upon the closure of Kingmoor at the end of 1967. *Britannia,* No. 70000, had already been withdrawn from Newton Heath in May 1966 and subsequently preserved.

There are more than 90 steam locos on Kingmoor this evening but over on the western side of the main line a diesel depot is under construction and this old Caledonian Railway depot will close in six months' time. All traces of the steam shed have today disappeared and the site is a nature reserve, fenced off from the main line.

43015

Now heading back to the station, attention is drawn to some steam activity at the south end of the shed and a K1 2-6-0 approaches, accelerating rapidly. No. 62044 is in a tremendous hurry but will have to slow down to negotiate the curves through the station. Another K1, No. 62026, is in steam at the north end of the shed, which has lost a sizeable portion of its roof, probably due to fire damage.

Opposite: After a long day it's now late evening on Day 1 of the Rail Rover and there is time for a rest back at Carlisle Citadel Station. Day 2 will be much longer, starting on the 00.02 train from Carlisle to Leeds and hoping to be asleep at Ais Gill Summit! Then it will be 02.37 Leeds—York, 03.57 York—Darlington, 05.15 Darlington—Thornaby and 05.41 Thornaby—West Hartlepool. The shed is, thankfully, a very short walk from the station and the locos in the roundhouse have certainly had a very quiet night – none are in steam. Ivatt Class 4 2-6-0 No. 43015 lurks in the shadows as the front end of Q6 0-8-0 No. 63394 dominates the foreground.

Church Street signal box is controlling the southern approaches to West Hartlepool Station, lack of ground space probably the reason for its elevated position. However, it will give good sight lines round the sharp reverse curves. Note the 'bobby' carefully observing the passage of a northbound coal train, hauled by Type 2 Bo-Bo No. D5150. He will be checking that the train is intact, an important part of a signalman's job, especially when loose-coupled freights were the norm. The freight lines to the nearby docks can be seen diverging to the right.

Back at the station, the next train is to be the 09.12 to Sunderland. After a short time, No. 62044 makes a surprise reappearance on a southbound freight, so its light engine trip must have been very brief. The severe curvature through the station was probably necessary to avoid the docks, which are hardly more than a stone's throw away to the right. The poster on the right advertising 'Snowcem' may bring back memories for older readers.

No. 62044 continues on its way south. A combination of the last two pictures gives a good impression of the layout of West Hartlepool Station and the severe reverse curvature. The Church Street box is visible in the distance, with the shed barely out of sight beyond.

Before moving on, a sobering thought: all the last four locomotives pictured, Nos. 43015, 62026, 62044 and 63394, will be withdrawn within a month. In fact, Nos. 43015 and 63394 were almost certainly withdrawn by the end of June, although this was not realised at the time.

The 09.12 to Sunderland is on time. This is train No. 13 since leaving Wigan and there has not been any significantly late running — yet!

It's now 09.50 at Sunderland as J27 No. 65892 heads north on a coal train. This station, on 30 June 1967, is no longer reminiscent of the steam age, as its rebuilding was only completed on 4 November 1965. The station opened on this site on 4 August 1879 was named Sunderland Central and the rebuilt station became simply Sunderland in May 1969. After No. 65892 has gone there is no sign of any more steam activity, so it's time to leave the station for a completely different experience — a bus ride to Philadelphia!

No. 42 is one of the famous 'Lambton Tanks' which came from a variety of sources, this one from Robert Stephenson in 1920, Works No. 3801. They were found to be ideal for the longer runs on the extensive network of industrial lines in the area, smooth riding with a good turn of speed. The massive coaling plant dominates this picture, an indication of the scale of steam operations based on the Lambton Locomotive Works at Philadelphia. At the time of this visit, there were at least 10 locos in steam in the vicinity.

Opposite: The timing of this visit to Philadelphia, approaching midday, is perhaps a little unfortunate, as many locos and crews appear to be taking their lunch break. However, loco No. 3 is receiving 'service with a smile' as a sandbox is refilled in preparation for the afternoon's work. A powerful 0-6-0 saddletank with outside cylinders, No. 3 ,is a relatively new loco, built by Robert Stephenson & Hawthorn in 1951, carrying Works No. 7687.

No. 8, an outside-cylindered 0-6-0 saddletank, built by Robert Stephenson & Hawthorn in 1952, Works No. 7691, fed and watered during its lunch break is now off to begin its afternoon's work. The level crossing is the focal point of the busy railway system at Philadelphia and its operation is apparently up to main-line standards. The North Eastern Railway was obviously involved in this installation, the signal on the right mounted on a slotted wooden post being a classic example of their practice. The sight of the refuse vehicle, typical of the period, waiting by the gates, will bring back memories to some readers!

Must catch the bus back to Sunderland now and then the 14.39 to Newcastle.

Steam has been reported at Bardon Mill Colliery, so, by catching the 16.25 Newcastle to Carlisle train, there is time to break the journey and investigate. Unfortunately, the loco, a very smart-looking Hawthorn Leslie 0-4-0 saddletank built in 1906, has been put to bed for the night in its small shed, making it impossible to photograph effectively.

Luckily a photograph can be taken when English Electric Type 4 No. D280 heads eastwards on a train of empty 21T hoppers, illuminated by the low, weak, evening sunlight. The very old signal box adds interest to the picture: built by the NER in 1874, it's quite small with only 21 levers.

On to Carlisle now and then the 19.28 to Preston, the 21.58 to Wigan and hopefully catch the last bus home. End of Day 2; it's been about 43 hours since getting up on Thursday morning!

ST

Day 4, Sunday 2 July, really is a day of rest. well, almost, as Day 5 will begin in the late evening by catching the 22.08 from Wallgate to Liverpool Exchange, then the 23.38 from Lime Street to York. This run, as far as Manchester, is the most uncomfortable and the most memorable journey of my life — on the footplate of BR 5MT No. 73140! The driver had evidently been watching my work with camera and tripod and to my great surprise asked, 'would you like to ride on the engine to Manchester?' It was immediately apparent during a laborious climb up to Edge Hill that No. 73140 was steaming very badly but a subsequent long delay at Earlestown was an opportunity for the driver to solve the problem. He broke up the large mass of clinker with the fire-irons when the fireman left to telephone the signalman (observing rule 55). He said nothing to his mate when he returned, who must have wondered why the engine now steamed perfectly! An enthusiast on the train claimed a sustained 76mph across Chat Moss, which certainly registered an enormous number of decibels on the footplate!

The delay resulted in a 56-minute late arrival in Manchester, but I was very pleased because it prolonged my footplate experience!

Opposite: The plan was to have a relaxing weekend and prepare for some intense activity on the final three days. However, it is with some reluctance that a shopping trip to Preston is agreed upon. While waiting for the intended train at the North Western Station, a Summer Saturday extra to Blackpool turns up, hauled by Black 5 No. 45375, and the staff assure us that it will stop at Preston. The driver, with nine coaches in tow is apparently in a great hurry to get out of Wigan and obviously has the full co-operation of the fireman. The pace quickens once over Coppull Summit and after a claimed 85mph near Euxton Junction, we have a non-stop run to Blackpool North!

The planned shopping in Preston is aborted; Day 3 has turned out very well!

English Electric Type 4 No. D253 now takes over at Manchester Victoria and arrives at York at 03.18, only seven minutes late and in good time to catch the 03.42 to Newcastle, which turns up on time, hauled by Brush Type 4 No. D1971. There is now a half-hour wait for the 05.52 to Sunderland, which is also on time and the arrival time at the shed is 06.45 in brilliant sunshine. Has it been worth losing a night's sleep?

There are at least 24 locos on shed, nine definitely in steam, and another four look condemned.

The roundhouse is full of J27s, most showing signs of life. No. 65879 is an early riser and it seems to have taken three men to move the turntable carrying its total weight of 84 tons. What is the equivalent horsepower? Three other J27s get into the picture: the preserved No. 65894, plus Nos. 65892 and 65811 which, built in May 1908, will be the oldest loco working on BR in August and September 1967.

No. 65879 is soon at work taking a short freight towards Ryhope Grange Junction. The complex of freight lines appears to be comprehensively signalled and there are at least two sizeable signal boxes in this vicinity. Is that gas lamp really in use in 1967? It certainly appears to be in full working order although it may be older than No. 65879, which dates from 1922.

Now looking towards the docks, a sign of times is the appearance of a diesel shunter, but some readers may find the signals far more interesting! The gantry carries some lower quadrant arms of NER origin and later upper quadrants controlling movements towards the docks. One of the signal boxes can be seen in the distance and now, down on the docks, No. 65879 has returned from its short trip working to assemble a train of empty 21-ton coal wagons before setting off to a local colliery. It's still a busy scene in July 1967 but some track in the right foreground over bridge No. 1 is already out of use and coal mining is in decline.

No. 65879 has now assembled a lengthy train of empty 21-ton hoppers and, still only moving at walking pace, heads towards Ryhope Grange Junction. This picture, looking south, complements the previous shot to complete the portrayal of this area, as it was taken from virtually the same spot. Another signal box can be seen in the distance, controlling mostly short-armed signals as commonly used in loops and sidings when the section ahead is not guaranteed to be clear.

There is now time to go back to the shed and photograph the preserved J27, No. 65894. It is the last of this class to be built, emerging from Darlington North Road Works in September 1923 and in common with the last 35 members of this class, it was originally superheated. Superheaters were later removed from most of these, including No. 65894 and 65879.

No. 65894 appears to be having a day off, with other J27s in steam: Nos. 65811, 65855, 65892 and of course 65879; also ready for work are at least four WDs: Nos. 90009, 90135, 90378 and 90417.

It's now time to get back to the station and catch the 09.42 to Newcastle.

Leaving Newcastle at 10.00 precisely, it's a short run to Tyne Dock. The shed appears to be quite run-down and only 18 steam locos are noted, at least eight of these looking condemned. Maybe the most interesting occupant is Service Locomotive No. 58, a J72 0-6-0T built by BR in November 1949. Numbered 69005, it escaped the cutter's torch in October 1964, starting a new life as Service Locomotive No. 58. It was then used when required, mainly for de-icing work around Tyne Dock. It's obviously in store in July 1967 and will be withdrawn before next winter, in October.

The J72 class has a remarkable history. A Worsdell design originating in 1898, further examples were built by Raven and even Gresley, the total number by the end of 1925 reaching 85. Quite remarkably, BR built another 28 between 1949 and 1951 with hardly any alterations to the original 1898 design, the class therefore totalling 113, built over a period of 53 years! No. 69023, which had also been in service as No. 59, is preserved and named *Joem.*

Note the preserved K1 No. 62005 in store behind No. 58.

The 11.22 from Tyne Dock back to Newcastle arrives punctually so there is time to refuel in the buffet before catching the 12.50 to Seaham. Unfortunately, steam activity, at this time at least, is much less than last year, so it's back to the station to see if there is anything interesting on the main line. Luckily, WD No. 90135, seen earlier in steam on Sunderland shed, is heading north on a coal train.

The signal box dates back to 1905 and has 23 levers plus the mechanism to operate the crossing gates. Safety measures include secure mechanical locking of the road gates and also the smaller pedestrian gates, all far more robust than the modern flimsy barriers. The box has windows at the rear and a mirror to aid sighting along the road. Note the gas lamp on the left.

Time to head back home now: 15.24 from Seaham, 17.25 from West Hartlepool, changing at Darlington for Manchester and then 20.25 to Wigan – all on time!

Opposite: Day 6, Tuesday 4 July, begins as Day 1 did, on the 05.45 Wigan North Western to Manchester Exchange, this time hauled by Standard Class 5 No. 73045, followed by the 06.46 Manchester to Leeds and the 08.40 on to Newcastle. At Newcastle, J27 No. 65882 enters the through road on the south side of the station and stops to take water at the western end. The station staff kindly allow me to cross some running lines and take some pictures. A timeless scene; this loco could have used the same NER water tower 44 years earlier!

65882

The appearance of No. 65882 at Newcastle is a bonus, as the main objective on Tuesday 4 July is investigation of the industrial steam activity north of the Tyne. The 11.05 to Backworth is on time and from there it's quite a long walk to Fenwick Colliery, about a mile to the north. Unlike virtually all locos on the main line, No. 39, in plain blue livery, is in immaculate condition and 0-6-0 outside-cylindered side-tank engines are not all that common at this time. No.39 was built by Hudswell Clarke in 1949, works No. 1824.

The wagons, for internal use only by the NCB, seem to be their equivalent of the 21-ton hoppers used on the main line.

Another mile to walk now to catch the 12.57 from Backworth to Wallsend, where it's only a short walk to the Rising Sun Colliery complex. Another outside-cylindered 0-6-0T, No. 38, is at work. Recent examination of photographs and notes (55 years later!) reveals that No. 38 is, maybe unsurprisingly, identical to No. 39 seen at Fenwick, although ever so slightly younger. It is Hudswell Clarke Works No. 1823 (No. 39 is 1824), built in 1949. No. 38 is seen taking water, the servicing facilities at Rising Sun appearing to be comprehensive and there are two spare locos in the shed.

No. 41 is also at work around the site. It is also a relatively new locomotive, an 0-4-0 saddletank built by Robert Stephenson & Hawthorn as late as 1951, Works No. 7674. Rising Sun began production in 1908, followed by large-scale coal preparation involving washing, blending and screening, the associated intensive shunting requiring two engines in steam. Just part of the huge works can be seen behind the loco.

However, the colliery closed on 26 April 1969, less than two years after these photographs were taken, so hastening the decline of steam in the area.

For some reason (I can't remember after 55 years) a bus is taken back to Newcastle, then the 15.20 to Sunderland, followed by another bus ride to Ryhope. At Ryhope Grange Junction, a sign of the times is the appearance of English Electric Type 3 Co-Co No. D6901 on a coal train. Although weighing in at 108 tons, it is judged to have insufficient braking power and therefore runs with a brake tender, a familiar sight at this time. It's probably a good idea since the darkening skies are threatening rain and the River Wear is not far beyond the buffer stops at the docks!

65879
65879

At Newcastle there is time, before boarding the train, to photograph Brush Type 4 No. D1520 waiting to leave on the 22.20 to York. The ghostly figures on the platform, staff dealing with parcels traffic, are created by their movements and a two seconds' exposure time. They are probably going to have a busy night dealing with the enormous piles of mail heaped on the trolleys.

Opposite: Before moving on, there is time for a final look at Ryhope Grange Junction and the magnificent signal gantry. The skies are still threatening rain but thankfully it stays dry as the old friend, J27 No. 65879, makes yet another appearance for the camera on its way once again to a local colliery with a train of empties. It's now early evening and it's going to be quite late by the time it gets back to the shed for the night. Time to catch a bus back to Sunderland.

The plan is to spend the night on various trains trying to get some sleep and get the earliest possible start on the final day. It's beginning to go dark by the time the 21.00 from Sunderland arrives in Newcastle.

Day 7, July 5, begins just after midnight at York and there is quite a long wait for the next train, at 02.10 to, surprisingly, Hebden Bridge! Staying awake at night is hungry work, but the buffet is found to be open for the night. A pork pie is a tasty snack in the early hours! The unmistakeable sound of a Deltic is heard and its source investigated. No. D9011 *The Royal Northumberland Fusiliers* is waiting to leave on the 01.12 to Kings Cross.

It's now time to locate the 02.10 to Hebden Bridge and, hopefully, settle down on the train to dose off for a while.

There is only a short time at Hebden Bridge before returning, as planned, on a Manchester to York train at 05.28, which arrives on time behind 'Peak' No. D33. The plan is to leave this train at Church Fenton but there is an unexpected long stop and an engine change at Normanton. During this time, the appearance of Stanier Class 4 2-6-4T No. 42574 shunting parcels vehicles at the rear of the train is of great interest. The 9E shed code (Trafford Park) is outdated and the chalked number on the smokebox door is actually 42574½. Could this be someone's clever way of indicating that this is one of the last two Stanier tanks? The other one, No. 42616, is at Low Moor at this time. Goose Hill Junction is beyond the bridge in the distance.

It's still early morning on 5 July at Normanton and Ivatt Class 4 2-6-0 No. 43084 has, unexpectedly, replaced No. D33 and will take the train to York. Note the steam-age gas lamps and signage as Black 5 No. 45075 runs by, heading to the shed.

Normanton Station was an important stop on the Midland Railway's route to Scotland before the introduction of dining cars. A prolonged stop was made here to allow passengers to use the buffet. Also, towards the end of the 19th Century, the island platform was reputed to be the longest in the world.

The shed is still operating steam; I should have investigated on Day 1 instead of going to Wakefield! The very dirty and run-down No. 43084 does make it to Church Fenton, although about 15 minutes late.

The late arrival at Church Fenton is of no consequence and the temptation to steam on to York is resisted. Plan A therefore continues by catching the 07.55 to Leeds, with a break at Micklefield to investigate steam activity at the nearby Peckfield Colliery. *Frank*, in sharp contrast to No. 43084, is in virtually immaculate condition and running very smoothly. It is 45 years old, built by Hawthorn Leslie in 1922 and obviously freshly overhauled. Peckfield Colliery, on the northern edge of the Selby coalfield, was sunk in 1872 and closed on 21 October 1980, thus ensuring the end of steam activity in this area.

The 09.14 from Micklefield is on time and before catching a train to Skipton there is time to photograph some steam at Leeds City. Fairburn 2-6-4T No. 42689 appears again now double-headed with Type 2 Bo-Bo No. D5177 moving down to attach to the Bradford portion of a train from Kings Cross. A 'Peak', which may have brought the train from London, also gets into the picture.

There's no more time to hang about; I must find the 10.25 Carlisle train.

There was no need to rush as it is 10.40 by the time the 10.25 leaves Leeds behind 'Peak' No. D23. At Skipton I must transfer to the 11.45 Carlisle 'stopper' to spend some time around Ribblehead and Blea Moor. No. D23 has arrived at Skipton only nine minutes late and the 11.45 is bang on time. At Hellifield both loops are occupied by 8Fs, No. 48261 on an up freight and No. 48646 likewise on the down side.

Not long after arriving at Ribblehead, Britannia No. 70024, formerly named *Vulcan,* appears on a southbound freight. Being unaccustomed to the weather in these parts, the sight of Whernside shrouded in low cloud in mid-summer is surprising!

Despite feeling rather tired after a sleepless night, Plan A must continue, i.e. a walk up to Blea Moor. Luckily, 8F No. 48646, seen earlier in the loop at Hellifield, appears on a northbound freight. It also seems to be very tired as it plods along over the viaduct and heads towards Blea Moor!

No. 48646 is a Lostock Hall loco at this time and is very likely to be working this train from the Preston area to Carlisle, a run of just over 100 miles but Blea Moor Tunnel will soon be in sight, marking the end of the really hard work.

Opposite: It seems a long way to Blea Moor in the warm, muggy, conditions. Britannia No. 70016, formerly named *Ariel,* is held in the down loop as 'Peak' No. D27 rushes past with a northbound express. No. 70016 will leave with a full head of steam to climb the last half-mile or so of the Long Drag up to Blea Moor Tunnel. The cluster of buildings near the signal box, most today gone, can be discerned despite the poor visibility. The water tower and the down loop are also consigned to history.

Back at Ribblehead Station, the on-time arrival of the 17.30 to Carlisle is a welcome sight. There is not much sight-seeing on this journey; it's almost impossible to stay awake!

1S 64

The final 100 miles of travel this week begins on the 19.28 from Carlisle to Preston, where transfer to the Wigan train is essential. Having dosed for most of the way between Ribblehead and Carlisle, will I be awake at Preston?

All is well, however, and the picture of Ivatt 2-6-0 No. 43119 warming sleeper coaches at Preston is a highly appropriate way to end the week's photography!

They will be attached to the 22.36 train to Euston after my departure on the 21.58 to Wigan, the 49th train of the week. All that remains is to catch up on sleep and, with some degree of anxiety, develop several films.

Chapter Seven Cumbria

In steam days, at the larger stations such as Carlisle, train spotters were entertained by the activities of station pilots shunting empty stock or parcels vehicles. An Ivatt Class 2 2-6-2T is on duty there on 9 August 1965. Note the two ex-LNWR ground signals, one pulled off for the reverse movement of No. 41229.

The LMS built the first 10 of this class at Crewe in 1946. Commencing with No. 41210, the rest were built by BR between August 1948 and May 1952, again at Crewe, except for the last 10 at Derby, bringing the total number to 130.

Allocated to Carlisle's Upperby shed at this time, No. 41229 was withdrawn on its closure at the end of 1966, the fate of many locos in that situation.

On 18 August 1966 Tebay and Shap stations are still open and the plan is, armed with a lineside photographic permit, to alight at Shap and spend the day walking to Tebay. Shap Station is about a mile north of the summit and southbound trains, after a short level stretch through the station area, face a climb of 1 in 106, before an easing to 1 in 130 before the summit.

Britannia No. 70041, formerly *Sir John Moore,* is making light work of the 1 in 106 with a parcels train and is now within sight of the summit.

There is a lot of freight traffic between Manchester and Carlisle, and Patricroft has turned out No. 73127, a Standard 5MT fitted with the Caprotti Valve Gear for one such working. Seen here at Shap Wells, it is making good progress on the upper stages of the climb with a 2-6-4T providing rear-end assistance.

The allocation of the 30 Caprotti 73XXXs is interesting. The first 20 went to Shrewsbury, Holyhead or Leicester, the last 10 to St. Rollox. By the summer of 1964 all the English examples were at Patricroft, where they stayed until withdrawal; all the Scottish locos were still at St. Rollox, but dispersed in Scotland before withdrawal. Nos. 73125, 73133, 73134 and 73143 were the last survivors, at Patricroft until June 1968.

Steam action is frustratingly elusive during the walk along the line from Shap Wells to Scout Green, where we are welcomed by the signalman. There is some good news; he's expecting steam on a southbound parcels train. It's not fake news and Lostock Hall Black 5 No. 45421 duly appears, the crew getting a cheery wave from the 'bobby'.

The crossing probably sees very little traffic at this time, sleepers sufficing for the roadway and it was later removed along with the box.

To many steam enthusiasts, 11 August 1968 may have seemed like the start of the 'dark ages' but there was still a great deal of industrial steam activity though in sharp decline and therefore well worth recording. On 3 April 1970 *J. N. Derbyshire*, an 0-4-0 saddletank built by Andrew Barclay, Works No. 1969, built in 1929, is working at the British Gypsum Cocklakes Works near Cumwhinton. It is seen crossing the Cumwhinton to Armathwaite road at an unprotected crossing, propelling a handful of wagons towards the works. The connection to the Settle and Carlisle line is at Howe & Co's. Siding, where the signal box is still in use although the sidings were lifted long ago.

HEADROOM
13FT.
ONLY
BEWARE
OF
LOCO
PARK CLEAR
OF LINES

In the early 1970s the NCB continued to operate a sizeable fleet of steam shunters and the Cumbrian coast was one of the main centres of activity. Now on four wheels, a day by the seaside is planned for 6 July 1970.

The first port of call is Lowca, near Parton, where Austerity 0-6-0ST *Amazon* is at work, a product of Vulcan Foundry in 1945, Works No. 5297. Seen from the western side of the Lowca complex, the industrial lines head north at a high level to Harrington, i.e. to the right in this picture. *Amazon* certainly appears to be in a precarious situation high above the Irish Sea, the Cumbrian Coast Line being out of sight at the bottom of the steep slope.

Opposite: Now at the works, where there is an extensive network of track providing access to all parts of the factory, the Barclay is having a busy afternoon's shunting. This picture illustrates the typical working conditions for industrial steam, the locos having to cope with a dirty environment and negotiate very uneven track.

This loco has been preserved, apparently carrying the name *Jane Darbyshire.*

About a mile south of Workington Station, industrial steam is seen in its natural habitat. Hudswell Clarke 0-4-0ST, Works No. 1814, built in 1948, is the workhorse for the day at Solway Colliery. In fairly typical industrial 'dirt' livery, it also looks as if there has been some D.I.Y. work on the cab to give the enginemen extra protection.

The huge British Steel plant provides an appropriate backdrop in 1970, but everything in this picture has now gone and there is even some greenery in the area.

Back to the seaside now, with a look at steam in the picturesque setting of Whitehaven Harbour on the same day, 6 July 1970. There is plenty of commercial shipping activity, evidently dealing mainly with coal and therefore involving rail transport. On the left, the presence of the *Marchon Venturer* is probably associated with the nearby Marchon Chemical Works. The *Ballyhill* on the right may be loading with coal for Ireland. An 0-4-0ST *Victoria*, engaged in shunting coal wagons, completes the picture. This loco was built at another west coast port, Bristol, in 1942 by Peckett, Works No. 2028.

Observed recently from a passing train, this area now appears to be a marina.

Moving round the dock, there is another 0-4-0ST at work on the same day, also dealing with coal traffic. The unnamed loco was built in 1942 by Robert Stephenson & Hawthorn, Works No. 7049 and was probably acquired at about the same time as *Victoria,* in the middle of the Second World War. The docks had their own engine shed, not far out of this picture to the left, where there was also a connection to the main line.

Opposite: The last picture of 6 July 1970 is taken at the Ladysmith coal grading and washing plant, situated about 1½ miles south of Whitehaven and connected by rail to Haig Colliery. *Revenge,* an Austerity 0-6-0ST built by Hunslet in 1950, Works No. 3699, is one of the locos later fitted with the Giesel Ejector exhaust system. The NCB seemed keen to fit this device to various types of locomotive. They must have found it advantageous, unlike BR whose sole experiment with 9F No. 92250 was regarded as a failure.

This picture also shows clearly just how uneven the track on industrial railways could be.

Before leaving Cumbria, here's a brief look at main line steam on Barrow shed back in 1966. By 12 July the number of Midland and LMS-built Jinties had greatly declined. Even by the end of 1965, only 86 out of the original 477 remained. No. 47373 is a comparatively late survivor, withdrawn in December 1966, leaving only four to soldier on into 1967. By the end of 1967 there were no standard gauge tank engines of any wheel arrangement running on BR.

Chapter Eight

A Summer Saturday Afternoon at Euxton Junction 4 July 1964

This photographic record of steam of steam passing through Euxton Junction on the afternoon of Saturday 4 July 1964 illustrates the reality of steam activity just more than four years before The End in Lancashire.

After an hour's bike ride from Wigan, the friendly signalman is shown my lineside photographic permit and he assures me that there will be plenty of steam in the next three hours.

It's not long before the 11.45 Blackpool to Manchester appears behind Black 5 No. 44732, scheduled to leave Preston at 13.01. With a load of nine coaches, it is immediately faced with a 1 in 128 climb as it leaves the junction. The safety valves are lifting, so the fireman has evidently prepared for the task ahead.

Not long after, the appearance of Fowler 2-6-4T No. 42374 on a train of empty stock is a welcome surprise. It has left Preston eight minutes after 44732, taking the coaches from Blackpool North to Wigan. It had worked the 09.06 from Eccles to Blackpool North this morning.

No. 42374, allocated to Stockport at this time, is to have a short spell at Springs Branch later, but this remains my only sighting of a Fowler tank on the West Coast Main Line.

There is a wait of barely 15 minutes before the Saturdays only Blackpool to Leicester appears hauled by Jubilee No. 45721 *Impregnable*. The pathing is interesting; along the slow line north of the junction and crossing over to the up fast after passing the junction, so keeping the Manchester line's connections to the fast lines clear in both directions.

45721 has had to negotiate the crossover at only twenty miles per hour and will now have to accelerate down a short length of 1 in 936 before the final climb to Coppull Summit, four and a half miles away, some of this at 1 in 114.

The appearance of a freight train on a summer Saturday afternoon is another welcome surprise. Crab 2-6-0 No. 42900 is heading north on a train described as 'banana empties'. As with the appearance of No. 42374, this is a most welcome sight, Crabs not being all that common on the main line by this time.

This class is often described as the 'Horwich Crab' but No. 42900 was, in fact, built at Crewe in August 1930.

Now moving north of the junction and a shot of the fastest train of the day! Black 5 No. 44856 is on a special working from Wigan to Blackpool Central and is taking full advantage of the straight alignment of the fast lines through the junction, no doubt maintaining this pace on the falling gradients to Preston unless checked.

The signals on the gantry, from left to right, apply to the following routes: up fast to Manchester, up fast main line, up fast crossing over to up slow (south of the junction). The right-hand group indicate up slow to Manchester, up slow to up fast main line and up slow main line. The ground signals control shunting movements through the trailing crossovers connected to the siding.

Not long after the high speed passage of No. 44856, Jubilee No. 45574 *India* appears on the 13.40 Manchester—Blackpool stopper. Travelling at the much more sedate speed of around 20mph, it threads its way across the whole layout to gain access to the down slow line. This crossover, for the use of trains on the Manchester line, replicates the one on the south side of the junction used by No. 45721 earlier.

The load is seven coaches, offering many more seats than similar services today.

At virtually the same spot the camera swings round to look north as Britannia No. 70039 *Sir Christopher Wren* storms through on a Glasgow—Euston relief. It was booked to pass through Preston at 14.26, so it's probably about 14.35 by now. No. 70039 is climbing at 1 in 432 at the moment, no problem with only nine coaches in tow, but Coppull Summit is 4½ miles away, so the fireman has been busy and now finds time to get a bit of fresh air.

There must be a chronic shortage of cleaners at Carlisle Kingmoor. If only the nameplates were cleaned, it would considerably improve appearances.

The external condition of another Kingmoor Britannia is no better than No. 70039. No. 70038 *Robin Hood* is coming off the Manchester line with the 14.00 Manchester to Glasgow and Edinburgh. Signalled to take the fast line, it will quickly accelerate once clear of the junction for a brisk run to Preston on falling gradients. The crossover traversed by No. 45721 earlier in the afternoon is in the foreground of the picture.

Now for something completely different — a clean engine! Jubilee No. 45675 *Hardy* has left Preston at 15.22 with the 14.25 Morecambe to Crewe, a train of only four coaches. Much earlier in the day it had worked the 06.16 from Crewe to Morecambe. It seems very likely that this is a running-in turn after overhaul at Crewe Works, which would also account for the light load. Holbeck Jubilees were always a good 'cop' at Wigan, only seen after their periodic visits to Crewe Works. No. 45675 was withdrawn from Holbeck in June 1967, leaving only three Jubilees in service: Nos. 45562, 45593 and 45697.

It is worth noting that all the 'namers' seen this afternoon are still carrying their nameplates, although this will not last much longer.

Finally, seen from almost the same spot, Black 5 No. 45013 takes the Manchester line with the 10.50 Edinburgh—Manchester relief, due to leave Preston at 15.28. The buffer stops on the right mark the end of sidings associated with the nearby Ordnance factory.

It's probably a quarter to four now and time to think about getting home for teatime. In just under 3 hours the amount of steam activity has exceeded all expectations. The tally is three Black 5s, three Jubilees, two Britannias, one Fowler 2-6-4T and one Crab.

Chapter Nine — Preston

This view of Preston Station has changed very little since 1966, even a Britannia making the occasional appearance! The signage has changed and the track in the right foreground connecting with the East Lancashire lines has gone, but the overhead wires are fairly unobtrusive. Britannia Pacific No. 70029, formerly named *Shooting Star,* is arriving with the 13.46 Barrow to Euston. No. 70029 is allocated to Carlisle Upperby at this time, September 1966, Kingmoor taking over this roster after the closure of Upperby at the end of the year.

There was usually some steam activity on the western side of the station, which was open to the public in steam days. Lostock Hall's Ivatt Class 4 Mogul No. 43029 is on pilot duties on 25 May 1967 as Black 5 No. 45092 prepares to leave on a southbound parcels train. The western island platform is today out of bounds to the public and No. 45092 is alongside the current Platform 1.

No. 43029 will be withdrawn from Lostock Hall in September 1967 along with another 5 43XXXs by the end of that year. A further six Ivatts would go in 1968, including the sole preserved example, No. 43106, the last survivor, in June.

The departure of heavy main line trains at the north end was guaranteed to provide some good entertainment. Black 5 No. 44680 is off to Blackpool and hasn't yet started its violent slipping as it enters Fishergate Bridge, requiring a rapid response from a very relaxed-looking fireman, who will soon have to operate the sanders. No. 44680, built at Horwich in June 1950, unusually spent all its working life at Crewe, on the North shed until May 1965, and withdrawn from the South shed in September 1967, only two months after this photograph was taken on 8 July.

Gas lamps appear on many pictures taken in the 1960s, but this one is perhaps the most surprising location and it does seem to be in full working order.

The intrusion of the diesels into the steam world can hardly be ignored in 1967. On 1 September Brush Type 4 No. D1855 is coming to a stop at Preston with a Birmingham to Aberdeen train. The staff have taken up a strategic position where they hope the parcels van will come to rest. A brief spell of frantic activity will follow, unloading first, then loading the mail bags, which are just arriving. All this done in an area fully open to the public! There will no doubt be a repeat performance at Lancaster.

Steam continued to operate between Preston and Carlisle in late 1967 and a good chance of getting a run over Shap is on a Manchester and Liverpool to Glasgow train. On 1 September hopes are pinned on the 14.30 departure from Preston, which duly arrives from Liverpool behind Britannia No. 70045, formerly named *Lord Rowallan,* with five coaches in tow. There are about 17 minutes to take water and do some shunting.

This is also a scene that has changed comparatively little since steam days, No. 70045 standing alongside the present Platform 2.

No. 70045 is now taking water at the north end. The fireman has initially used the ladder to climb onto the back of the tender, but obviously can't descend by that route! The driver is wondering where he is and eventually climbs down to turn off the impressive cascade of water himself, as the fireman escapes by scrambling over the coal bunker into the cab.

After assurance from the driver that the engine is working through to Carlisle, it's time to dash off and book a ticket for a first-ever steam run over Shap. Another six coaches have arrived from Manchester to make up an 11-coach train.

The departure from Preston is a couple of minutes late and the run to Lancaster takes 25 minutes from start to stop. Hopes of a non-stop run from Lancaster to the booked stop at Penrith are dashed when steam is shut off on the approach to Tebay. The banker, believed to be BR Standard Class 4 No. 75027, is seen about to buffer-up to the rear of the train. The weather is worsening, so maybe the driver is simply taking no chances.

A comparison of this September 1967 run with a run behind *Scots Guardsman* on 9 May 2009 with an almost identical 11-coach load is very interesting: Oxenholme—Grayrigg, pass to pass: No. 70045 13 minutes, No. 46115 8 minutes 10 seconds; Tebay—Shap Summit: No. 70045 10 minutes 45 seconds, No. 46115 6 minutes 45 seconds. Total time Oxenholme—Shap Summit: No. 70045 35 minutes 30 seconds, 46115 20 minutes 20 seconds. This certainly highlights the achievements of all involved in the operation of main line steam in the preservation era.

Back to Preston now for a look at some exotic steam on 14 October 1967. The LCGB, North West Branch, organised the 'Castle to Carlisle' rail tour, offering a complex route from Liverpool Exchange, hauled by 9F No. 92091 via Southport, Wigan Wallgate, Horwich Fork Junction and Chorley. No. 7029 *Clun Castle* took over at Preston for the run to Carlisle. The down departure from Preston is difficult for steam and the three rear coaches of the train seem to be on the short 1 in 101 section immediately north of Fishergate Bridge. This tour included a ramble around Carlisle behind Ivatt Mogul No. 43121, 7029 returning via Ais Gill to Hellifield, where No. 92091 was on hand to return the train to Liverpool Exchange.

Chapter Ten The Blackburn Area

This substantial viaduct spans the River Darwen just under a mile west of Pleasington Station. Black 5 No. 45231 is running briskly towards Preston on 17 July 1968, not long before The End. It will be seen later on Lostock Hall shed, even though it is allocated to Carnforth at this time.

No. 45231 will be one of the 46 Black 5s to remain on the stock list until August, and has done a lot of main line running in preservation.

The weather forecast is not good for 16 July 1968, but as it's so near The End this must not be a deterrent to photography. The platforms are wet at Blackburn, but it is not raining as 8F No. 48423 coasts though with a coal train from Yorkshire.

The enormous size of the 'train shed' is shown to good effect in this shot, the roof on flexible mountings to allow for expansion and contraction as temperature fluctuates.

Unfortunately, the weather forecast is correct and by the time 8F No. 48775 arrives with a short pick-up freight, it's raining quite heavily. Numerically 48775 is the last of the 8Fs, but it was built relatively early, in April 1937, at Crewe. It entered WD service in the Second World War and was purchased by BR in September 1957 along with 48773 and 48774. It acquired its large top-feed cover in its WD days and retained this until withdrawal in August from Lostock Hall.

TO PLATFORMS
1 TO 5
PLATFORM
7
GENTLEMEN

On 16 July 1968, getting some decent pictures at Blackburn in the dull, wet weather is becoming increasingly challenging, so just one more picture before calling it a day. At least the camera can be kept dry under the canopy as 8F No. 48493 heads a train of coal empties eastwards towards the Yorkshire coalfield.

The station was rebuilt by the LYR between 1886 and 1888 and was virtually unchanged at the end of steam, rebuilding to its present form taking place in the year 2000 by which time even the gas lamps had been replaced.

Opposite: It's now time to shelter under the canopy as the weather worsens. Black 5 No. 45156, which had been standing near the south end, has had to make way for the 8F to do its shunting. There is now no trace of 45156's former name *Ayrshire Yeomanry*.

The presence of a DMU and No. 45156 dates this picture, taken in the much older setting of the LYR station which nevertheless had basic facilities in all areas. The layout of this station was basically two island platforms with bays at both ends. There are today just four platforms, including one bay at the south end.

Before leaving Blackburn, here are a couple of pictures taken almost two years earlier. What *is* the time at Blackburn on this day in September 1966? There are three clocks on view, all showing different times! The two nearest the camera probably date back to LYR days and almost agree; the more modern one on the left seems to have moved forward into a slightly more advanced time zone. 8F No. 48187, a Springs Branch loco, is working a coal train from Parkside Colliery to the nearby Whitebirk power station.

Both these platforms were retained after rebuilding, the DMU standing at the current number four and No. 48187 passing through number three.

Opposite: A bit later on the same day in September 1966, a WD 2-8-0 makes a welcome appearance. No. 90625, a Wakefield loco, is heading a train of coal empties into Yorkshire and will be among the last WDs working in England on withdrawal in May 1967. All the WDs working in England at this time are on the North Eastern Region, with other survivors in Scotland. The large cab-side numbers have been applied after overhaul at Darlington.

Blackburn Tunnel burrows under part of the town and No. 90625 will emerge near Daisyfield Junction. The splitting distant signals indicate the route set at the junction, in this case to Accrington and Burnley, the lower arm applying to the Hellifield line. The small arm below is used to allow shunting movements within the station area.

J.OSBALD'STON

A momentous day in the history of steam preservation is 1 April 1967, the first run of A4 Pacific No. 4498 *Sir Nigel Gresley.* The weather, however, shows no respect for this and it's cold and wet as No. 4498 climbs the 1 in 82 gradient through the closed Wilpshire Station. The outward run from Crewe to Carlisle had been quite sensational, topping 90mph after leaving Crewe, followed by a very fast ascent of Shap. The weather deteriorated during the day and the return over Ais Gill proved far more difficult.

The abiding memory of this occasion is watching sparks coming off the spinning driving wheels as No. 4498 slithered up to the summit, the sand boxes probably empty by this time.

Chapter Eleven East Lancashire

Overleaf: The summit of the Blackburn to Clitheroe line is at Wilpshire and northbound trains can coast down the four miles to Whalley on a gradient of 1 in 82. On Sunday 4 August 1968 the focus of attention will be on the steam specials due to pass through Blackburn later in the day. However, Brush Type 4 No. D1735 is the first sighting of the day, working a train diverted off the main line to head north through Settle to Carlisle, seen here emerging from Wilpshire Tunnel.

The passengers may well appreciate the run through the picturesque Ribble Valley, a line promoted by the LYR as their scenic route.

The English Electric Type 4s seem to be increasingly regarded as mixed traffic locomotives in the later 1960s. On 17 July 1968, No. D227, named *Parthia,* is climbing out of the Ribble Valley about half a mile south of Langho on the 1 in 82 climb to Wilpshire on a fitted freight. Home of witches, the famous Pendle Hill, is visible in the background and No. D227 is coping with the gradient without a banker.

Bankers were stationed at Whalley, the lowest point on the Blackburn to Hellifield line, to give assistance if required up to Wilpshire. On 18 June 1967 a heavy freight is probably expected as Black 5 No. 45421 waits in the siding by the signal box, a typical LYR structure.

At Lostock Hall there has been some attempt to brighten up the front end of 45421, which was last seen returning from Carlisle on a parcels train at Scout Green on 18 August 1966. The station at Whalley is closed at the time of this picture, but reopened in May 1994 and there is now a regular service from Clitheroe to Rochdale.

It's a busy scene at Clitheroe on 16 February 1967. Fairburn Class 4 2-6-4T No. 42297 has been shunting the yard and is almost ready to return towards Blackburn after the fireman, in a seemingly very precarious position, has finished the watering. These passenger tanks have never been a common sight on freight work, but there were virtually no suitable passenger jobs available to them by this time. There are some brake-fitted vans at the front of this train, a welcome increase in braking power with these locos on freight work.

8F No. 48313 is working a freight from Brindle Heath to Carlisle and may have stopped to detach some empty cement wagons.

Opposite: On 15 October 1967 an E.E. Type 4 No. D224 *Lucania* has arrived at Whalley with a Long Meg—Widnes anhydrite train. It is evidently unable to cope with the gradient and stops to take the banker; the wet weather maybe an excuse for this precaution. Black 5 No. 44800 is certainly doing its share of the work as they set off over the viaduct, already on the start of the gradient.

Whalley viaduct, built mainly of distinctive red brick, is a 48-arch structure, always referred to locally as 'Whalley Arches'.

There were extensive sidings and two goods sheds at Clitheroe dating back to the 19th Century when the railways were the principle overland freight carriers. By the mid-1960s, however, due mainly to competition from road transport, the decline of this traffic is looking terminal. On 2 November 1967, Rose Grove 8F No. 48081 is shunting the yard and the demolition of one of the goods sheds is well underway, to be eventually replaced by a supermarket; the 8F is in the future car park.

A little later on 2 November 1967, No. 48081 moves vigorously through the south end of the yard amid this scene of dereliction. The old, still gas-lit, goods shed on the left is probably disused by this time and is also ripe for demolition. It still needs to shunt the coal siding, which runs through the steam-age cobbles in the foreground.

The cement wagon in the background is a reminder of the continuing importance of this traffic to the nearby Ribble Cement Works, now called Castle Cement. This is now dealt with at Horrocksford, with no need for any shunting near Clitheroe Station.

On 23 February 1968 another Rose Grove 8F, No. 48348, is engaged in the daily shunting at Clitheroe. There seems to have been a problem with a cement wagon, which it has shunted into a siding for inspection. The station has been closed to passengers for about six years at this stage, but fortunately the main buildings have been left intact and are still in non-railway use at the time of writing.

No. 48348 is nicely posed by the signal box, which was of some historical interest, being one of the older boxes on BR. It was almost certainly the same age as the existing boxes at Daisyfield, Blackburn and Horrocksford, both dating from 1873, built by Saxby & Farmer for the LYR and both earmarked for preservation.

In those far-off youthful days, it was possible to dash up to the castle and get a bird's eye view of the shunting. No. 48348 is now attached to a rake of coal empties and will pick up the cement wagons before departure. At this time coal is delivered by rail to the cement works, the gasworks and the goods yard for collection by the local coal merchants. The gasworks dominates this part of the town in 1968 but is perhaps outdone by the parish church and the castle, which are on higher ground; it has now been replaced by housing and a car park.

After the departure of the 8F there is time to investigate railway operations in the gasworks, resulting in a surprising discovery. The shunting had been done by an electric locomotive until recently and the overhead catenary is still in place. The electric loco, built by English Electric in 1928, Works No. 737, is lying out of use and a Ruston Hornsby diesel shunter, seen on the left, has taken over. The overhead wires are visible, as is the vantage point for the previous picture up at the castle. It must have been possible to see steam, diesel and electric traction at Clitheroe, maybe not long before this date, 23 February 1968.

There was steam shunting at Clitheroe right up to the last days of steam on BR. Frustratingly, the exact date of this final picture, taken in the last week, was not noted, but is likely to have been on Friday 2 August 1968. The driver of 8F No. 48723 kindly allows me onto his footplate and to photograph him at work. His intense concentration is evident as he gently buffers up to an empty 21T coal hopper. It's a long way to the front of an 8F and a rough shunt may cause a derailment or injury to men on the ground.

A sad day: steam in regular service will not be seen in Clitheroe again.

Two different forms of steam power are active at Huncoat Colliery and the nearby power station on 8 August 1966. The conventional coal-fired 0-4-0ST, named *Raven*, built by Hawthorn Leslie in 1935, Works No. 3800, is busy at the colliery. The loco is perhaps in better shape than most industrials, having a cover over the slide bars to protect against dirt and apparently even a seat for the driver! The first wagon, although labelled 'Internal use only' will be used to deliver coal to the nearby power station, outside the confines of the colliery, but without using the main line.

Fireless locomotives were commonly used at thermal power stations where there is a ready supply of superheated water to charge the 'boiler', more accurately described as the steam accumulator. The steam accumulates above the hot water and, with good insulation, the heat is retained for long time, depending on the amount of work done.

Both locos were built by Bagnall in 1951. No. 2, near the camera, is Works No. 3022, and No. 1, Works No. 2989, is feeding the coal drops in the background.

At Accrington the gas light under the station canopy is still burning on the very dull, wet morning of 24 April 1967. Fairburn Class 4 2-6-4T No. 42187, a loco last seen at Standish Junction almost three years earlier, is running light engine back to its home shed at Lostock Hall to face a very uncertain future.

The setting is almost pure LYR as No. 42187 needs more than a whiff of steam to keep moving on the sharp check-railed curve.

Is this its last outing? Withdrawal is to be before the end of the following month, May 1967.

Before leaving Accrington, here is a glimpse of steam on a uniquely busy day, 17 March 1968. William Deacon's Bank Club organised two identical tours from Stockport to Carnforth, both involving locomotive changes at Accrington. The first has arrived behind *Flying Scotsman* and Black 5 No. 45290. The A3 has been replaced by Black 5 No. 44899 and this train is now leaving for Skipton. No. 4472 will turn on the triangle after taking water and then run tender-first light-engine to Skipton, followed by a forward run to Carnforth, reunited with the train.

The second train is a repeat performance with *Oliver Cromwell* and Black 5s Nos. 45447 and 45110. The triangle is a remnant of the junctions with the line to Bury, closed on 3 December 1966, and is partially dismantled at this time. The Skipton line was severed at Colne early in 1970.

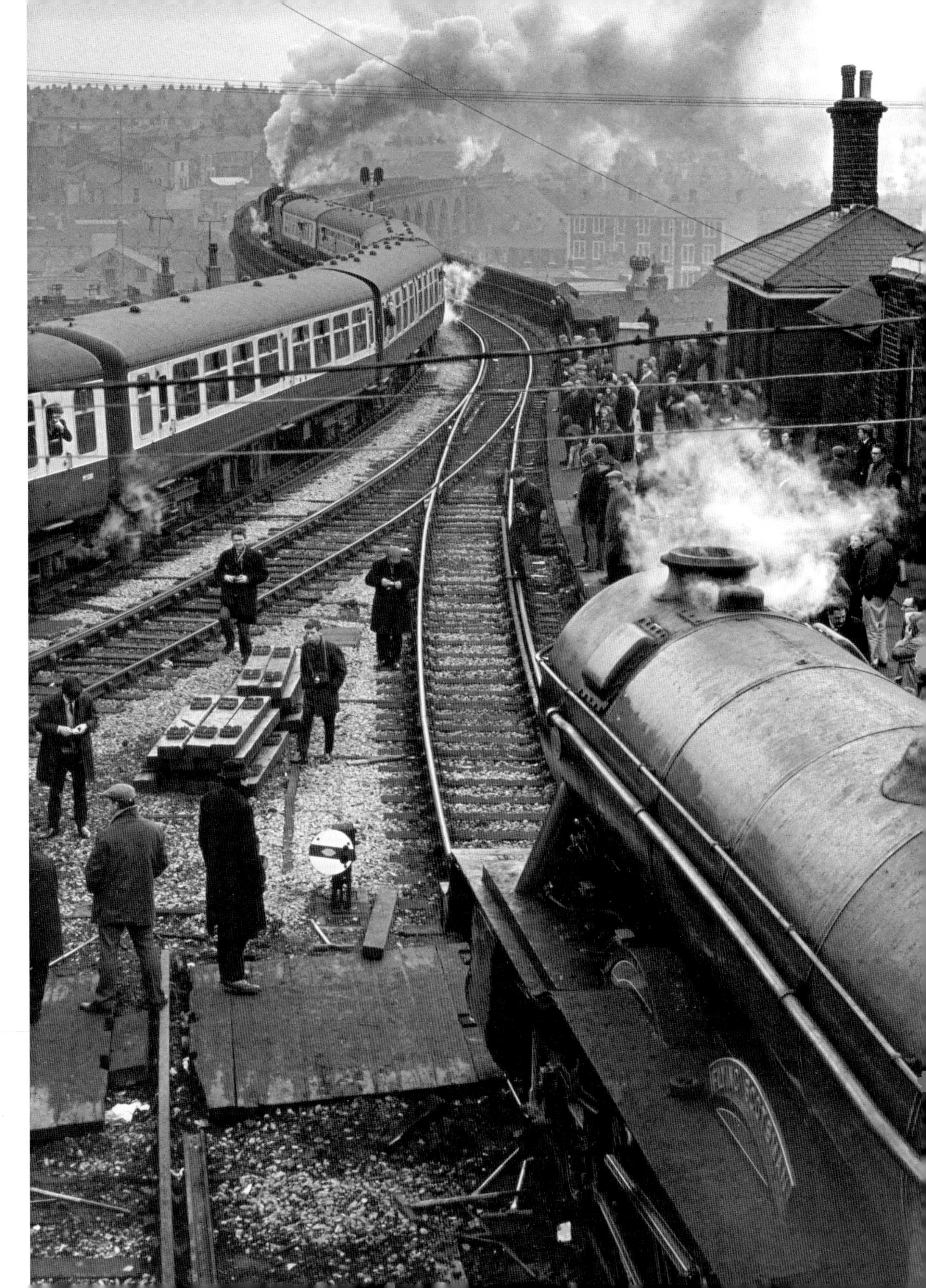

Chapter Twelve Epilogue

It seems that most of the enthusiasts seen at Blackburn have also converged on Ais Gill Summit on the following Sunday! BR now considered steam power to be obsolete, but would this massive public response to the 'last rites' be sufficient to persuade them to relax their proposed ban on main line steam?

The 'Fifteen Guinea Special' had left Liverpool Lime Street behind Black 5 No. 45110, with 70013 taking over at Manchester Victoria for the run to Carlisle. The return run to Manchester, again over Ais Gill, was hauled by Black 5s Nos. 44781 and 44871, 45110 then returning the train to Lime Street.

Opposite: There will never be another day at Blackburn like Sunday 4 August 1968. The last scheduled steam-hauled passenger train, the 21.25 from Preston to Liverpool Exchange, had run on the previous day and five of the six trains commemorating this event are to pass through Blackburn. Eleven locomotives are involved: Black 5s Nos. 44781, 44871, 44874, 44894, 45017, 45156 and 45407; 8Fs Nos. 48476 and 48773; Britannia No. 70013 *Oliver Cromwell,* and BR 5MT No. 73069.

The 1Z74 is an LCGB tour from St. Pancras to Carnforth, arriving at Blackburn behind No. 70013 and 44781. No. 48773 has replaced No. 70013 for the run to Carnforth, carrying a headboard reading 'Farewell Rose Grove Steam' and a wreath transferred from *Oliver Cromwell* as the pair, observed from crowded platforms, head towards Blackburn Tunnel.

The purchase of *Flying Scotsman* by Alan Pegler and its subsequent main line running was one the most important developments of the 1960s. No. 4472 is seen here on 15 May 1965 climbing the 1 in 132 gradient out of Carlisle at Durran Hill. It is returning from Dumfries, via Settle, to Lincoln Central on a tour organised by the Gainsborough Model Railway Society.

In retrospect, the increasingly popular rail tours that ran right up to The End can be seen as portentous events; the presence of 4472 on the main line probably the most significant of these. BR had agreed to allow *Flying Scotsman* to run a limited number of rail tours after August 1968 and it was even seen at Kings Cross on 21 September, as well as on 6 and 20 October 1968. However, enthusiasts had to wait until 1980 for the revival of regular main line steam rail tours in the summer months.

On the 54th anniversary of the "Fifteen Guinea Special", 11 August 2022, main line steam operation is to be on a scale which nobody could possibly have envisaged in 1968. There will be steam in Mallaig, Settle, Carlisle, London Victoria and Canterbury on this day and some of the locomotives involved only narrowly escaped the cutter's torch in 1968!

Index

Numbered Industrial Locomotives with Locations:

Named Industrial Locomotives with Locations:

Main Line Steam Locomotives by Number:
***Named or formerly named locos**

Main Line Electric and Diesel Locomotives

Named locos:

Locations: